MAPS • GLOBES • GRAPHS

Writer

Henry Billings

Consultants

Gloria Sesso
Dix Hills, New York

Edna Whitfield
St. Louis, Missouri

STECK-VAUGHN
C O M P A N Y

A Division of Harcourt Brace & Company

www.steck-vaughn.com

D1298096

Acknowledgments

Editorial Director	Diane Schnell
Project Editor	Janet Jerzycki
Design Manager	Rusty Kaim
Electronic Production	UG/GGS Information Services, Inc.
Media Researcher	Claudette Landry
Cover Design	Donna Neal
Cartography	Land Registration and Information Service
	Amherst, Nova Scotia, Canada
	Gary J. Robinson
	MapQuest.com, Inc.
	R.R. Donnelley and Sons Company

Photo Credits

Cover images courtesy of Cartesia Software; p. 4 ©Victor Brunelle Photography, Inc/Stock Boston; p. 5(t) ©Jeffrey Dunn/Stock Boston; p. 5(b) ©PhotoDisc; p. 6 ©Jim Steinberg/Photo Researchers; p. 7(t) ©Kaz Chiba Photography/Liason International; p. 7(b) ©PhotoDisc.

Illustration Credits

Dennis Harms pp. 8, 9, 10, 11, 12, 13, 50, 71, 78; David Griffin p. 79 inset, p. 80 inset; Michael Krone p. 42 inset; Rusty Kaim p. 4

ISBN 0-7398-0979-2

Printed in the United States of America. 1 2 3 4 5 6 7 8 9 0 DP 05 04 03 02 01 00 99

Contents

Geography Themes 4

1 • Globes 8

2 • Symbols and Directions 14

Geography Themes Up Close:
  Movement 20

3 • Scale and Distance 22

4 • Route Maps 28

Geography Themes Up Close:
  Place 34

5 • Relief and Elevation 36

6 • Latitude and Longitude 42

Geography Themes Up Close:
  Location 48

7 • Climate Maps 50

8 • Combining Maps 56

Geography Themes Up Close:
  Human/Environment
  Interaction 62

9 • Comparing Maps 64

10 • Time Zones 70

Geography Themes Up Close:
  Regions 76

11 • Projections 78

12 • Graphs 84

Atlas 92

Glossary 95

Standardized Test 97

Answer Key 101

To The Learner

Maps•Globes•Graphs is a series of three books designed to help you learn the skills necessary for understanding and using maps, globes, and graphs. Since you will be working with maps directly on each page, you will get lots of hands-on experience. You should find this experience helpful when you read road maps, atlases, and a variety of the kinds of charts and graphs you find in newspapers and magazines.

Each of the chapters in this book focuses on one skill. The first eleven chapters deal with map and globe skills. The last chapter focuses on skills needed to read bar graphs, circle graphs, line graphs, and tables.

In addition to the chapters, you will find a few other features in this book. On pages 92–94 are atlas maps of the United States and the world. You may find these as well as the glossary on pages 95 and 96 handy references. On pages 97–100 there is a sample standardized test. This test covers many of the skills in the book. Its main purpose is to familiarize you with a standardized test format. If you are a student, you will probably take a test similar to this one some time in the future. The answer key is on pages 101–107. The answer key provides the answers to all of the questions in this book. Following the answer key are five different outline maps that you can use to practice the skills you learn in the chapters.

As you work through this book, you will take a trip around the world. Enjoy your trip!

Geography Themes

In *Maps•Globes•Graphs* you will learn about some of the tools that scientists use to study **geography**. Geography is the study of Earth and the ways people use Earth to live and work. There are five themes, or topics, to help people organize ideas as they study geography.

The Five Themes of Geography
- **Location**
- **Place**
- **Human/Environment Interaction**
- **Movement**
- **Regions**

Location

Location describes where something can be found. One way to describe the location of something is to use an address. Another way is to name what something is near.

 Based on what you see in this photograph, describe the location of Jackson Middle School.

_____

_____

Place

Place describes the **physical features** and **human features** of a location. The physical features of a location are natural features that include the climate, landforms, soil, bodies of water, and plants and animals. The human features are those made by people, such as population, jobs, language, customs, religion, and government.

 How would you describe
Rio de Janeiro, Brazil?

_____

_____

_____

Human/Environment Interaction

Human/Environment Interaction describes how the environment affects people and how people affect the environment. This theme also describes how people depend upon the environment. For example, some people depend on lakes to provide them with drinking water.

Human/Environment Interaction describes how people adapt to their environment.

 The people in this photograph live in Egypt, which has a hot, dry climate. How do you think their clothing helps them adapt to their climate?

_____

_____

_____

Human/Environment Interaction also describes how people change the environment to meet their needs and wants. Some changes may be harmful to the environment. For example, clearing land of all trees may cause soil erosion. Other changes people make can be beneficial.

 How are irrigation systems helpful in areas of little rain?

_____

_____

_____

Movement

Movement describes how and why people, goods, information, and ideas move from place to place. Movement is often described in terms of transportation and communication. Highways, railroads, and rivers are examples of transportation networks that move people and goods from place to place. Television, newspapers, and computers are examples of communication tools that move information and ideas from place to place.

 Explain the kind of movement represented in this photograph.

_____

_____

_____

Regions

Regions describe places on Earth with similar features. Physical features, such as landforms, natural resources, or climate can describe a region. The Amazon River basin is a region defined by its physical feature—the Amazon River. Human features, such as politics, religion, customs, or language, can also describe a region. Canada is a region described by political divisions called provinces. Regions can be large, such as the Eastern Hemisphere, or small, such as a neighborhood.

 How would you describe the region shown in this photograph? List a physical or human feature that defines the region.

_____

_____

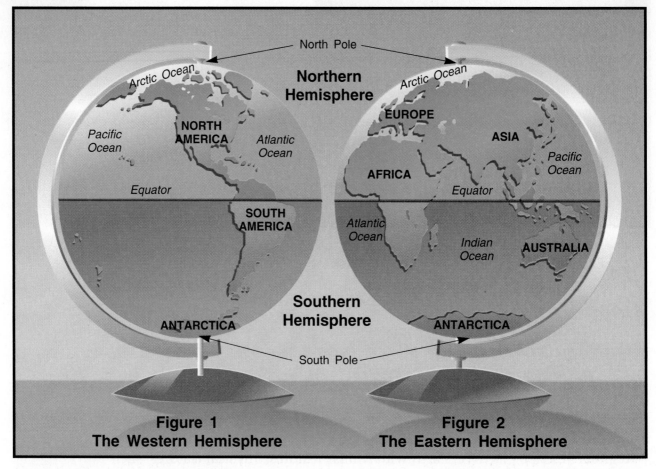

Figure 1
The Western Hemisphere

Figure 2
The Eastern Hemisphere

A **globe** is a model of Earth, which is shaped somewhat like a sphere, or ball. Globes show **continents** and **oceans**, the large land and water masses on Earth. Find the seven continents and four oceans on Figures 1 and 2 above.

Some points and imaginary lines help us find places on Earth. The **North Pole** and the **South Pole** are the places farthest north and south on Earth. We use the poles to know the four main directions, north, south, east, and west.

Find the **Equator** on Figures 1 and 2. This imaginary circle around the middle of Earth divides Earth into two hemispheres. **Hemisphere** means half a sphere or globe. The hemisphere north of the Equator is called the **Northern Hemisphere**. The hemisphere south of the Equator is called the **Southern Hemisphere**.

The globe can also be divided into the **Eastern Hemisphere** and the **Western Hemisphere**. Figure 1 shows the Western Hemisphere. Figure 2 shows the Eastern Hemisphere.

► If you stand on the North Pole, what is the only direction you can go?
If you stand on the South Pole, what is the only direction you can go?

► Name the seven continents and the four oceans.
Which continents and oceans are in the Eastern Hemisphere?
Which are in the Western Hemisphere?

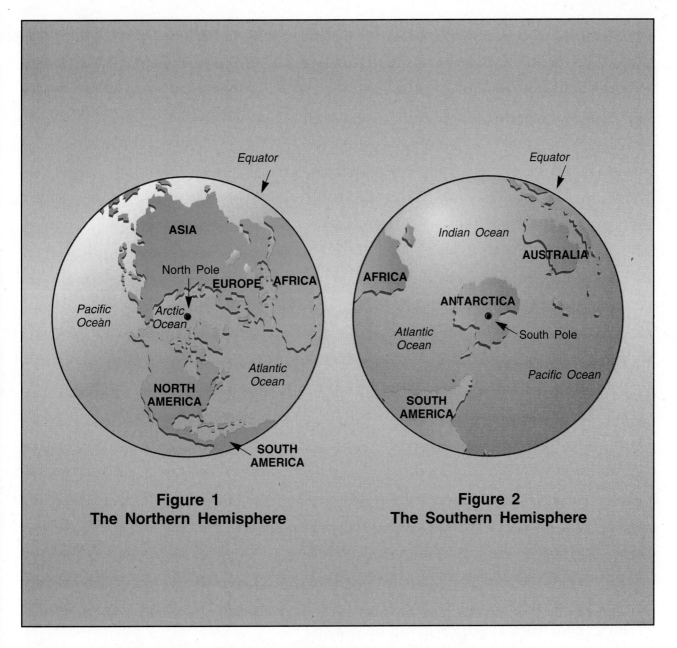

Figure 1
The Northern Hemisphere

Figure 2
The Southern Hemisphere

Figures 1 and 2 show a different way of looking at the Northern and Southern Hemispheres. Figure 1 shows the Northern Hemisphere with the North Pole in the center. What continents do you recognize? Look back at the hemispheres on page 8 to help you identify the continents.

Figure 2 shows the Southern Hemisphere with the South Pole in the center. The South Pole is on which continent? What other continents do you see?

► Can you find the Equator on both Figure 1 and Figure 2?

► Which oceans are in the Southern Hemisphere? Which are in the Northern? Which continents are entirely in the Southern Hemisphere? Which continents are entirely in the Northern Hemisphere? Which have parts in both the Northern and Southern Hemispheres?

► Most of the land is in which hemisphere? Most of the water is in which hemisphere?

Mastering the Eastern and Western Hemispheres

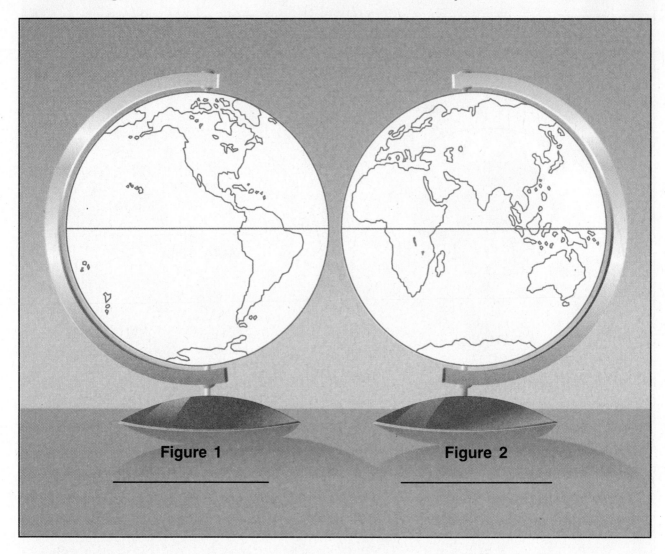

Figure 1

Figure 2

1. Label the Eastern and Western Hemispheres on the lines under Figures 1 and 2. Look back at page 8 if you need help.
2. Label the North Pole, South Pole, and Equator on each globe.
3. Label the continents and oceans on Figures 1 and 2. Again, look back at page 8 if you need help.
4. Which two continents are entirely in the Western Hemisphere?

   _____

5. Which four continents are entirely or mostly in the Eastern

   Hemisphere? _____

   _____

6. Which continent is almost evenly divided between the Eastern and

   Western Hemispheres? _____

7. Which ocean is entirely in the Eastern Hemisphere? _____

Mastering the Northern and Southern Hemispheres

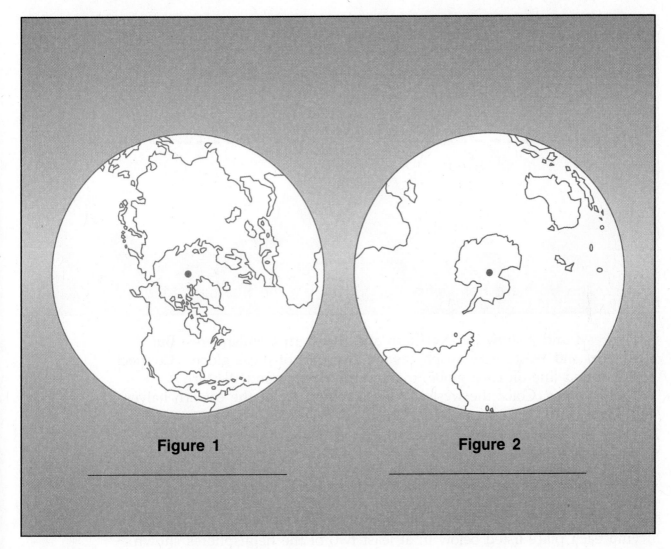

Figure 1

_____

Figure 2

_____

1. Label the North Pole, the South Pole, and the Equator on each globe. Look back at page 9 if you need help.
2. Label the Northern and Southern Hemispheres on the lines under Figures 1 and 2.
3. Label the continents and oceans on each hemisphere.
4. From the South Pole, the only direction you can go is _____.
5. From the North Pole, the only direction you can go is _____.
6. Which two continents are only in the Southern Hemisphere?

   _____

7. Which three continents are only in the Northern Hemisphere?

   _____

8. Draw an arrow pointing from South America to Africa on Figure 2.

   Which direction is that arrow pointing? _____

Mastering the Four Hemispheres

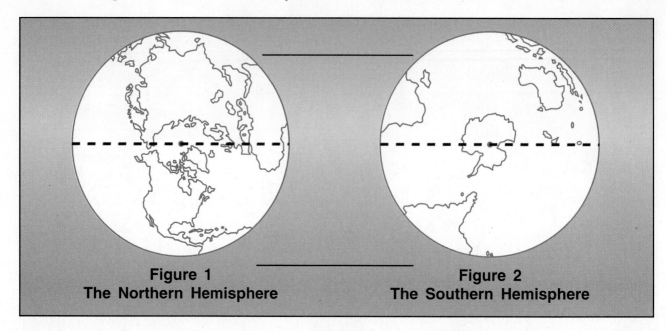

Figure 1
The Northern Hemisphere

Figure 2
The Southern Hemisphere

1. Figures 1 and 2 show the Northern and Southern Hemispheres. But the Eastern and Western Hemispheres are also part of these globes. Connect the dotted line on each globe to show the Eastern and Western Hemispheres. Color the western halves yellow. Color the eastern halves orange.

2. Label the Western Hemisphere and Eastern Hemisphere on the lines where they belong.

3. What point is at the center of the Northern Hemisphere? _____

4. What point is at the center of the Southern Hemisphere? _____

5. Find each place listed below in at least two of the hemispheres shown above. Some continents and oceans are in three or four hemispheres. Name the hemispheres in which you find each place.

   a. North America: _____

   b. Pacific Ocean: _____

   c. Arctic Ocean: _____

   d. Europe: _____

   e. Atlantic Ocean: _____

   f. Australia: _____

   g. Indian Ocean: _____

   h. Africa: _____

   i. Asia: _____

✓ Skill Check

Vocabulary Check

North Pole	South Pole	globe
Equator	hemispheres	oceans
continents		

Write the word or phrase that makes each sentence true.

1. The _____ is the place farthest north on Earth.

2. The Equator divides Earth into two _____.

3. A _____ is a model that shows the shape of Earth.

4. Earth's _____ and _____ are large land and water masses.

Globe Check

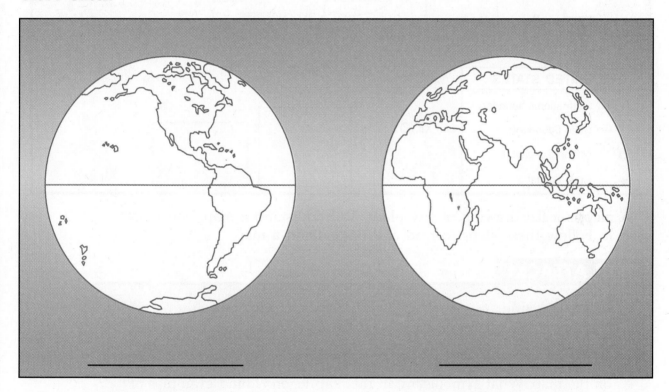

_____   _____

1. Label the hemispheres you see. Then label the continents, the oceans, the poles, and the Equator on each globe.

2. Which three continents are closest to the North Pole? _____

_____

3. Besides Antarctica, which three continents are closest to the South Pole?

_____

4. What point on Earth is farthest from the North Pole?

_____

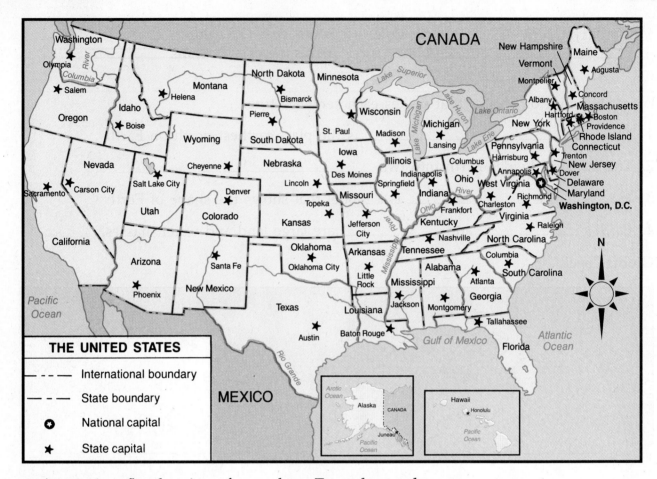

A **map** is a flat drawing of any place. To understand a map, you must read it. Follow these steps to read and understand a map.

MAP ATTACK!

- **Read the title.** Just as a book's title tells you what you are reading, a map's title tells you what the map shows. What does this map's title tell you?
- **Read the map legend.** The legend, or key, explains the symbols on the map. What symbols are in the map legend? Find examples of each symbol on the map.
- **Read the compass rose.** The compass rose always shows north. The north arrow points to the North Pole. Once you find north you can find the other **cardinal directions**, east (E), west (W), and south (S). The compass rose often shows the **intermediate directions**: northwest (NW), southwest (SW), northeast (NE), and southeast (SE). Find the compass rose on the map. Then find each direction.

► From the capital city of Kentucky, in what direction is the capital of each of these states: Indiana, South Carolina, Ohio, Virginia, Tennessee, and Florida?

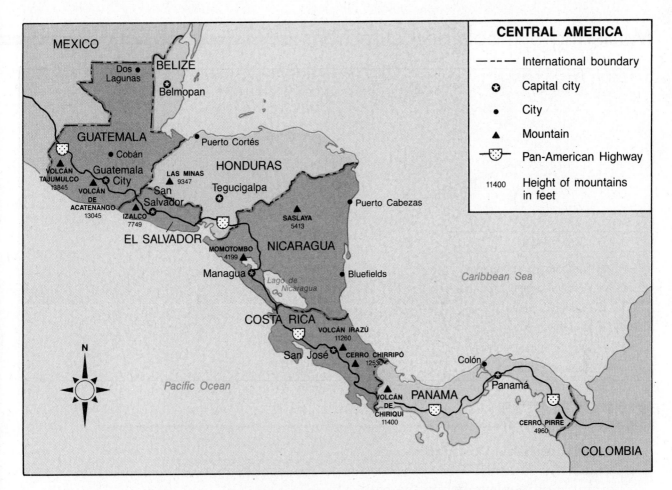

Not all maps show the same information. The title tells you the kind of information you can learn from the map. The legend explains the special symbols used on the map. Follow the **Map Attack!** steps to understand the information on this map.

MAP ATTACK!

- **Read the title.** What part of the world is shown on this map?
- **Read the legend.** What major highway is shown on this map? What kind of landform is shown?
- **Read the compass rose.** Where is the North Pole from Central America?

Notice on the map above that the labels are not all the same size. Labels for the largest places on a map are usually large and sometimes are shown in all capital letters. Labels for water are often blue.

► What countries make up Central America?

► The Pan American Highway crosses which countries?

► Which country has the highest mountains? How high are they? How do you know?

► Which mountain is farthest east?

Mastering Symbols and Directions

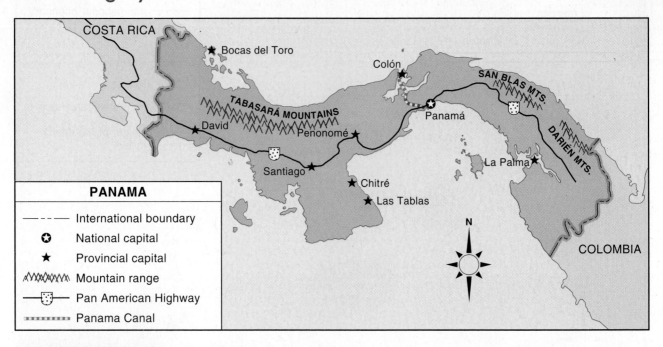

MAP ATTACK!

- **Read the title.** This map shows _____.
- **Read the legend.** What symbols are in the legend? Find an example of each symbol on the map.
- **Read the compass rose.** Find north. Then label the remaining points.

1. Label these bodies of water. Look back at page 15 for help.

   Caribbean Sea   Pacific Ocean

2. What country borders Panama on the east? _____

3. What country borders Panama on the west? _____

4. How many mountain ranges are shown on the map? _____

5. Find these pairs of places on the map. What direction would you travel to get from the first place to the second place? Write the abbreviation of the correct cardinal or intermediate direction.

   a. Bocas del Toro to David   _____

   b. Santiago to Penonomé   _____

   c. the national capital to La Palma   _____

   d. Colón to Chitré   _____

   e. Las Tablas to Santiago   _____

6. Is the Pan American Highway north or south of the mountain ranges? _____

Mastering Symbols and Directions

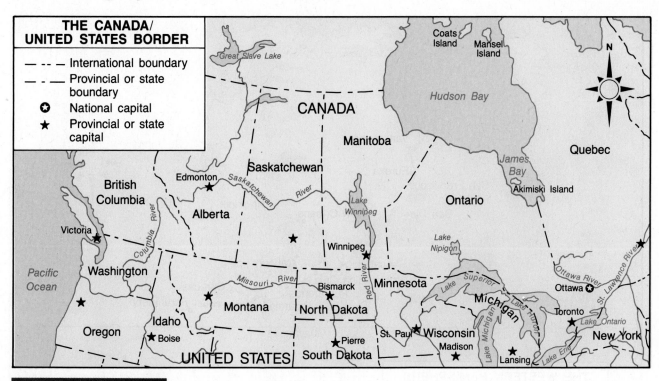

MAP ATTACK!

Follow the steps on page 16 to begin reading this map.

1. Trace the boundary between Canada and the United States in red.
2. Trace the state and province boundaries in green.
3. Label these capital cities.

   Salem, Oregon   Regina, Saskatchewan
   Quebec, Quebec   Helena, Montana

4. Victoria, British Columbia, is on Vancouver Island.
   Label Vancouver Island.
5. What state and province does the Columbia River flow through?

   _____

6. What large lake is in central Manitoba? _____
7. Lake Superior forms a boundary for what states and province?

   _____

8. What island is in James Bay? _____
9. What direction would you travel to get from Lansing to Toronto? _____

   From Manitoba to Alberta? _____
10. The Red River forms a boundary between what two states?

    _____

Mastering Directions on a Map

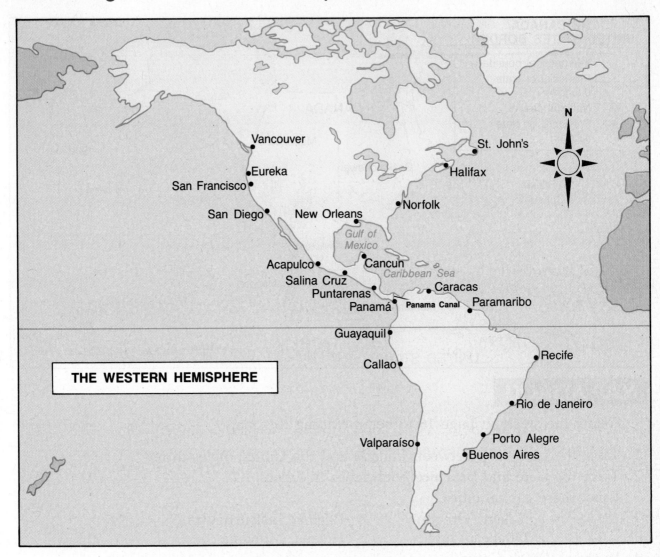

1. Write the following labels where they belong on this map.

   NORTH AMERICA   SOUTH AMERICA   CENTRAL AMERICA
   ATLANTIC OCEAN   Equator   PACIFIC OCEAN

2. Plan an ocean cruise along the western coast of North America. Begin in Vancouver. Name, in order, four other port cities on your route.

   _____

3. Sail from the western coast to the eastern coast through the

   Panama Canal. What body of water do you enter? _____

4. Continue sailing south along the eastern coast of South America. Name, in order, four port cities along this route.

   _____

5. Trace your route from Vancouver to Buenos Aires in red. Circle the cities on the route.

✓ Skill Check

Vocabulary Check
     map   title   compass rose
     intermediate directions   legend   cardinal directions

Write the word or phrase that best completes each sentence.

1. A _____ is a flat drawing of a place.

2. North, south, east, and west are _____.

3. You can find north on a map by looking at the _____.

4. The map's _____ explains the map's symbols.

5. The map's _____ tells you what the map shows.

Map Check

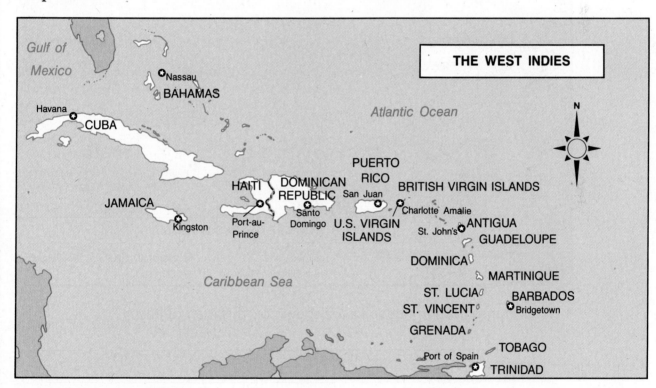

1. Highlight each of these countries using a separate, light color.
        Cuba   Jamaica   Haiti   Dominican Republic

2. On the map, draw an arrow from the first place to the second place in each pair. In which direction does each arrow point? Write the correct abbreviation for each direction below.

   Nassau to Havana _____   Dominican Republic to Haiti _____

   Bridgetown to St. Vincent _____   Jamaica to Antigua _____

   San Juan to Charlotte Amalie _____   Trinidad to Tobago _____

Geography Themes Up Close

Movement describes the ways that people, goods, information, and ideas move from place to place. How do you get to and from school? Where do goods that you buy come from? How do you know what is going on in your community and in other parts of the world? These kinds of questions are answered in the study of movement. Movement happens through transportation and communication.

TRANSPORTATION NETWORKS IN RUSSIA

1. What transportation networks are shown on this map of Russia?

   _____

   _____

2. According to the map, how do people in Murmansk get goods to Vladivostock?

   _____

   _____

3. What means of transportation connects Russia's east coast with its western border?

   _____

4. Based on the map, in what part of Russia would it be most difficult to transport people and goods? Why?

_____

_____

Charts show facts organized and arranged in columns and rows. The chart below shows the number of some communication tools in various countries.

Communication Tools In Selected Countries

Country	Number of televisions per 1,000 people	Number of radios per 1,000 people	Number of newspapers per 1,000 people
Bolivia	202	560	69
China	189	177	23
France	579	860	235
Libya	105	191	15
Russia	379	341	267
United States	776	2,122	238

5. Which two countries have the fewest communication tools per 1,000 people?

_____

6. How might the information in the chart help geographers study the movement of information and ideas ?

_____

_____

_____

3 Scale and Distance

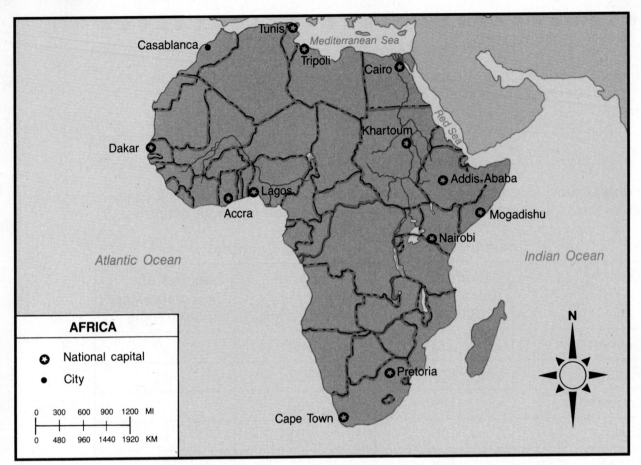

AFRICA

⊙ National capital

● City

| 0 | 300 | 600 | 900 | 1200 | MI |
| 0 | 480 | 960 | 1440 | 1920 | KM |

Maps can show the actual shape of a place. They cannot show the actual size of a place. The size of the place must be reduced to fit on a piece of paper. To help us figure distances, maps are drawn to scale. Scale is used to keep the shape of a place <u>and</u> show the distances. On the map of Africa above, the scale is "1 inch = 1,200 miles or 1,920 kilometers." A **map scale** shows the relationship of the actual distance on Earth to the distance on a map.

Map scales often show distance in miles (MI) and kilometers (KM). Find the map scale on the map above.

Miles and **kilometers** are two units of length used to measure distance. In the United States, distances are usually measured in miles. In many other countries the usual measurement is kilometers.

Find Dakar and Accra on the map of Africa above. They are only one inch apart. But how far apart are they on Earth? To find out, use the map scale and a ruler, a string, or the edge of a paper to figure the number of miles or kilometers between Dakar and Accra. The distance is about 1,200 miles or 1,920 kilometers.

► What is the distance between Khartoum and Addis Ababa?
Find the distance in miles and kilometers.

► What is the distance between Tripoli and Cape Town?
Find the distance in miles and in kilometers.

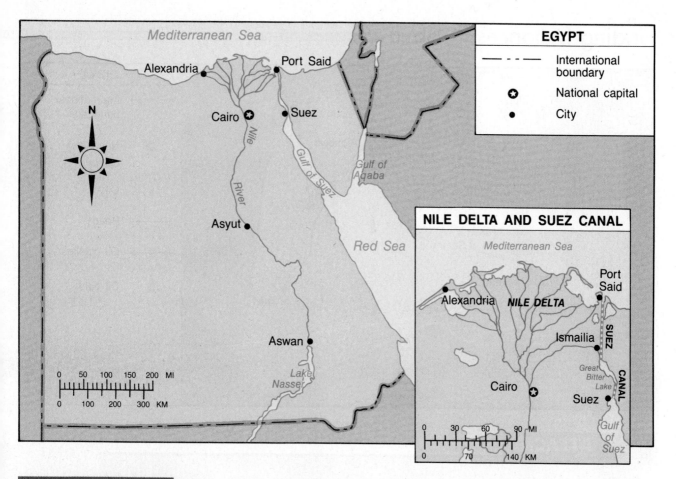

MAP ATTACK! Add a step to read the maps.

- **Read the title.** What can you learn from these maps?
- **Read the legend.** Find each symbol on the maps.
- **Read the compass rose.** Find north on each map.
- **Read the map scales.** How does the scale differ on each map?

The scale is not the same on all maps. Look at the two maps above. The larger map shows all of Egypt. The smaller map is an inset map that shows only part of Egypt: the Nile Delta and the Suez Canal. An **inset map** is a small map within a larger map. An inset map may have its own scale.

► Compare the scales on the two maps.

► Measure the distance between Suez and Port Said on the map of Egypt. What is the distance?

► Measure the distance between Suez and Port Said on the inset map. What is the distance?

► On which map is it easier to measure distances?

► Can you measure the distance between Ismailia and Asyut? Why or why not?

► How could you figure the distance between Ismailia and Asyut using both of the maps?

Finding Distances in Libya

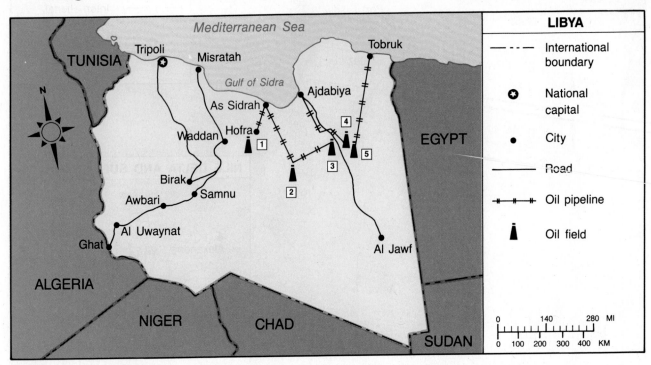

MAP ATTACK!

- **Read the title.** This map shows _____.
- **Read the legend.** Check (✔) each symbol in the legend and a matching symbol on the map.
- **Read the compass rose.** Complete the compass rose.
- **Read the map scale.** The length of the scale stands for how many miles _____? how many kilometers? _____

1. Trace each oil pipeline. Then find its length.

   a. Hofra to As Sidrah   _____ KM _____ MI

   b. Oil field #2 to As Sidrah _____ KM _____ MI

   c. Oil field #4 to Ajdabiya   _____ KM _____ MI

   d. Oil field #5 to Tobruk   _____ KM _____ MI

2. a. Which oil pipeline covers the longest distance?

   _____

   b. Which oil pipeline covers the shortest distance?

   _____

3. Draw a conclusion. Where do all the oil pipelines in Libya go?

   _____ Why? _____

Finding Distances in Southern Africa

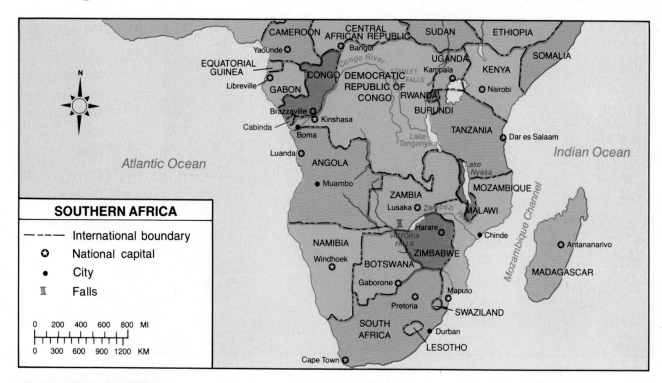

MAP ATTACK!

Follow the steps on page 24 to begin reading this map.

1. Draw a line from the first place to the second. Then find the distance.

   a. Cape Town to Windhoek _____ KM _____ MI

   b. Windhoek to Kinshasa _____ KM _____ MI

   c. Kinshasa to Bangui _____ KM _____ MI

   d. Bangui to Kampala _____ KM _____ MI

   e. Kampala to Nairobi _____ KM _____ MI

   f. Nairobi to Maputo _____ KM _____ MI

   g. Maputo to Cape Town _____ KM _____ MI

2. What is the total distance of this trip? _____ KM _____ MI

3. Trace the Congo River from Stanley Falls to Boma.

   Use the map scale to estimate this distance. _____ KM _____ MI

4. Trace the Zambezi River from Victoria Falls to Chinde.

   Use the map scale to estimate this distance. _____ KM _____ MI

5. Which river trip is longer? _____

Finding Distances in Northern Africa

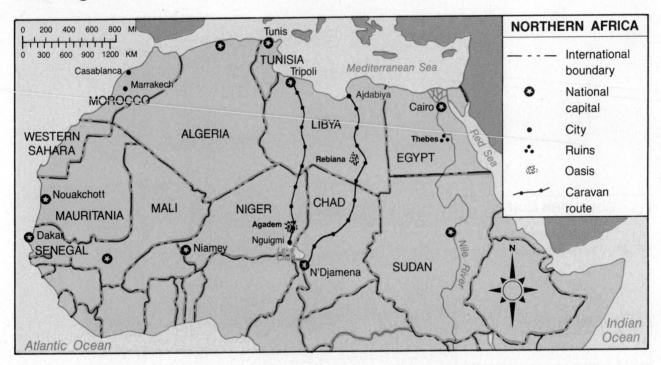

1. The Mediterranean Sea is a boundary for what countries? _____

   _____

2. Label these capital cities.
   a. Algiers, Algeria
   b. Khartoum, Sudan
   c. Bamako, Mali

3. Trace the caravan route from Tripoli, Libya to Nguigmi, Niger.

   a. What direction does it go? _____

   b. What oasis does it pass by? _____

   c. From Tripoli to Nguigmi is about _____ KM or _____ MI

4. Find the distance between the following cities and the direction from the
   first city to the second.

	Distance		Direction
a. Casablanca to Marrakech	_____ KM	_____ MI	_____
b. Nouakchott to Tunis	_____ KM	_____ MI	_____
c. Dakar to Cairo	_____ KM	_____ MI	_____

5. How far are the ruins at Thebes from Cairo? _____KM _____MI

6. If a camel went 40 kilometers a day, how long would a trip by

   camel from Cairo to the ruins take? _____

Skill Check

Vocabulary Check   **map scale**   **inset map**   **miles (MI)**   **kilometers (KM)**

1. To show the relationship between the actual size of a place and its

   reduced size on a map, map makers use _____.

2. Distances in the United States are usually measured in _____.
3. Distances in countries other than the United States are usually

   measured in _____.

Map Check

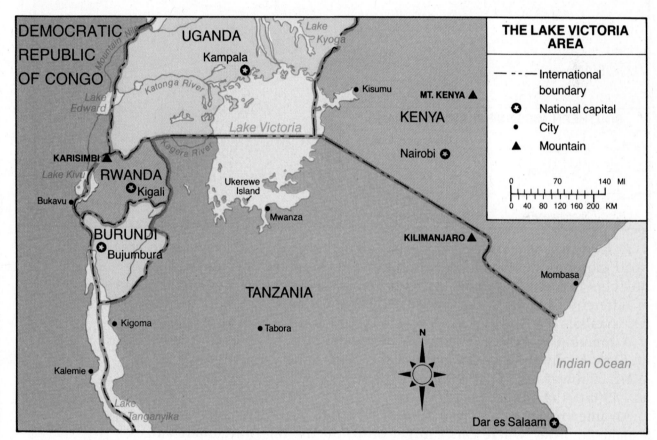

1. About how long is the border between Kenya and Tanzania?

   _____ KM   _____ MI
2. Find the distance between these places.

   a. Nairobi to Mombasa   _____ KM   _____ MI

   b. Dar es Salaam to Kigali   _____ KM   _____ MI

   c. Kampala to Bujumbura   _____ KM   _____ MI

   d. Mt. Kenya to Kilimanjaro   _____ KM   _____ MI

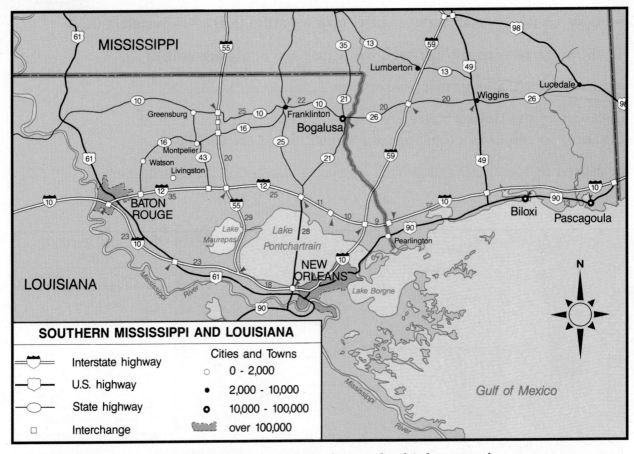

SOUTHERN MISSISSIPPI AND LOUISIANA

Interstate highway	Cities and Towns	
U.S. highway	○	0 - 2,000
State highway	●	2,000 - 10,000
Interchange	◉	10,000 - 100,000
		over 100,000

A road map is a kind of route map that shows the highways of an area. Road maps show several kinds of highways. Most major roads have numbers to identify them. This road map also has special symbols for cities of different sizes. Read the legend to learn the meaning of the highway and city symbols.

A **junction** is a place where two highways cross or meet. Put your finger on State Highway 26 at the right of the map. Slide your finger to the left along Highway 26. What is the first highway you cross? Where Highways 26 and 49 cross is a junction.

An **interchange** is a special kind of junction. An interchange is a place on a major highway where cars can get on or off the highway. Interchanges have special connecting ramps to allow vehicles to change roads without interrupting the flow of traffic. Find an interchange on Interstate 12.

Find the red numbers on the map between junctions and cities. These **mileage markers** give the distance in miles between each set of red triangles. What is the distance between Biloxi and Pascagoula on U.S. 90?

► Which city is larger, Biloxi or Pearlington?

► What body of water do Interstate 10 and Interstate 12 go around?

► Where is the junction of State Highway 25 and State Highway 10?

► If you got off Interstate 59 south of Lumberton, what highway would you be on? What is the first city you would come to going west?

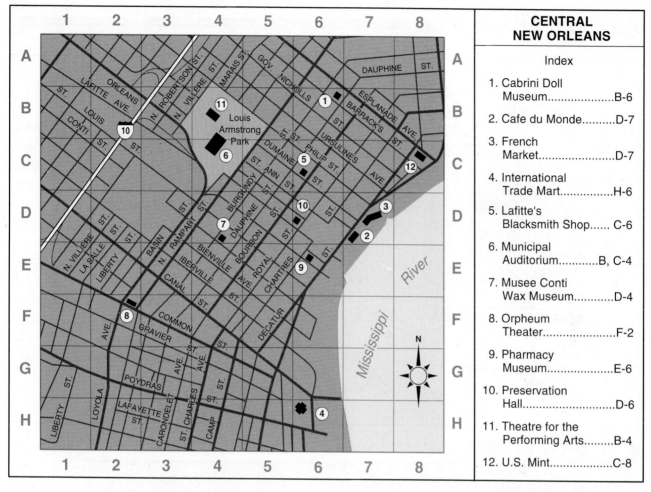

CENTRAL NEW ORLEANS

Index

1. Cabrini Doll Museum....................B-6

2. Cafe du Monde..........D-7

3. French Market.....................D-7

4. International Trade Mart...............H-6

5. Lafitte's Blacksmith Shop...... C-6

6. Municipal Auditorium............B, C-4

7. Musee Conti Wax Museum............D-4

8. Orpheum Theater.....................F-2

9. Pharmacy Museum...................E-6

10. Preservation Hall...........................D-6

11. Theatre for the Performing Arts.........B-4

12. U.S. Mint..................C-8

A street map is also a route map.

Maps often have grids. A **grid** is a pattern of lines which cross to form squares on the map. With a grid, it is easy to find places on the map. Each square in the grid is labeled with a **coordinate**. The rows of squares are labeled with a letter. The columns are labeled with a number. Each individual square has coordinates of a letter and a number. The **map index** lists places alphabetically with their grid coordinates. If you know the name of a place, and you want to find it on the map, begin by looking in the index. Find the Pharmacy Museum in the index. What are the coordinates for the Pharmacy Museum? Now find the row labeled E on the map. Slide your finger across the row until you come to column 6. Find the Pharmacy Museum in that square.

► Find Louis Armstrong Park on the map.
  What two buildings are located in this park?
  What street borders the park on the east?

► Find the Cabrini Doll Museum on the map.
  What other buildings are in that column?

► Use the map index and grid to find these places on the map.
    Cafe du Monde   Preservation Hall   Orpheum Theater

► What places could you visit if you walked southwest on Decatur from the U.S. Mint?

Reading a Route Map

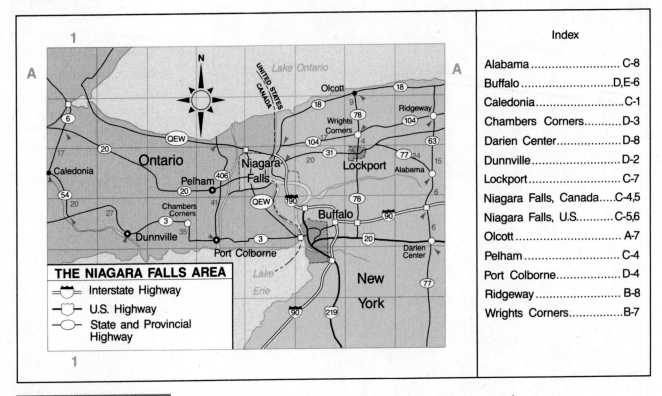

Index

Alabama C-8
Buffalo D,E-6
Caledonia.........................C-1
Chambers Corners...........D-3
Darien Center....................D-8
Dunnville..........................D-2
Lockport...........................C-7
Niagara Falls, Canada.....C-4,5
Niagara Falls, U.S...........C-5,6
Olcott A-7
Pelham C-4
Port Colborne..................D-4
Ridgeway B-8
Wrights Corners...............B-7

MAP ATTACK!

- **Read the title.** This map shows _____.
- **Read the compass rose.** Label the intermediate direction arrows.
- **Read the grid and index.** Finish labeling the grid rows and columns.

1. Put an X on Niagara Falls, U.S.A. Put an O on Niagara Falls, Canada.

2. What highway enters Niagara Falls, U.S.A., from the north? _____

3. If you left State Highway 20 at the first junction out of Niagara Falls and

   drove south, what city would you come to? _____

4. a. What highway goes along the north shore of Lake Erie?_____

   b. In what city could you turn north to Lake Ontario? _____

5. Circle the interchange on Interstate 90 just south of Alabama. If you
   exited I-90 at that interchange and drove north 21 miles, what city would

   you come to? _____

6. What highways form a junction at Ridgeway? _____

7. Where would you see this sign?

Niagara Falls	20
Wrights Corners	4
Alabama	24

_____

Reading a Route Map

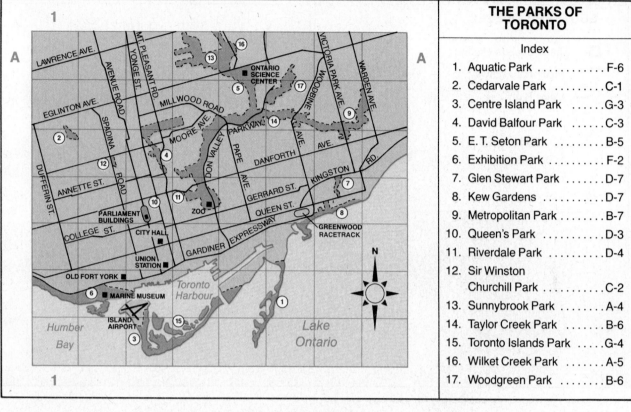

THE PARKS OF TORONTO

Index

1. Aquatic Park F-6
2. Cedarvale Park C-1
3. Centre Island Park G-3
4. David Balfour Park C-3
5. E. T. Seton Park B-5
6. Exhibition Park F-2
7. Glen Stewart Park D-7
8. Kew Gardens D-7
9. Metropolitan Park B-7
10. Queen's Park D-3
11. Riverdale Park D-4
12. Sir Winston
    Churchill Park C-2
13. Sunnybrook Park A-4
14. Taylor Creek Park B-6
15. Toronto Islands Park G-4
16. Wilket Creek Park A-5
17. Woodgreen Park B-6

1. Complete the grid by adding the missing letters and numbers.
2. Name each park described.

   a. just south of Wilket Creek Park _____

   b. in the same grid square as Woodgreen Park _____

   c. with the Parliament buildings _____

   d. at the corner of Moore Avenue and Spadina Road

   _____

   e. on the southern end of Woodbine Avenue _____

3. What two parks are on the same island as the Island Airport?

   _____

4. What parks border the Don Valley Parkway? _____

   _____

5. What street is east of Metropolitan Park?

   _____

6. What streets would take you from Woodgreen Park to Sir Winston

   Churchill Park? _____

Reading a Route Map

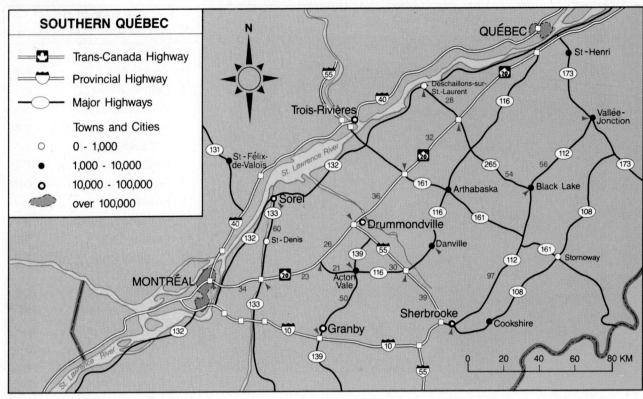

1. What highway takes you from Granby to Acton Vale? _____

2. a. How many kilometers is it from Acton Vale to the interchange just

      south of Granby? (Read the mileage marker.) _____

   b. Use the map scale to measure the distance "as the crow flies"
      (in a straight line) from Acton Vale to the interchange just south of

      Granby. The distance is _____ kilometers.

   c. Why do you think the distances differ? _____

3. a. What is the distance "as the crow flies" from the interchange on

      Highway 55 southeast of Drummondville to Granby? _____

   b. What is the distance along the highways? _____

4. a. Where is the junction of Highways 112 and 265? _____
   b. If you drove 54 kilometers northwest of that junction, what junction

      would you come to? _____

5. a. What highway goes along the southern shore of the St. Lawrence River?

      _____

   b. Where would you exit that highway to get to Black Lake?

      _____

Skill Check

Vocabulary Check   junction   interchange   grid
                       coordinate   mileage marker   index

Write the word or phrase that best completes each sentence.

1. A _____ is the place where two roads meet or cross.

2. An _____ is a junction of major highways and has special connecting ramps or roads.

3. A _____ indicates distance between cities.

Map Check

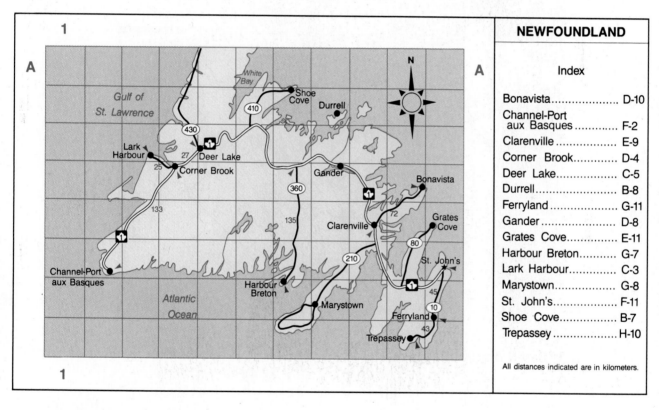

1. Complete the map grid by adding the missing letters and numbers.
2. Name each place described below.

    a. a city at the junction of Highways 1 and 430 _____

    b. a city 88 kilometers south of St. John's _____

    c. a city 25 kilometers northwest of Corner Brook _____

3. Where do you leave Highway 1 to go to Bonavista? _____
4. Which highways would take you from Harbour Breton to Shoe Cove?

_____

Geography Themes Up Close

Place focuses on the physical and human features of an area. Is the climate humid and wet or cold and dry? Are there mountains, hills, lakes, or rivers? How are the people governed? What language do they speak? The answers to these kinds of questions describe place.

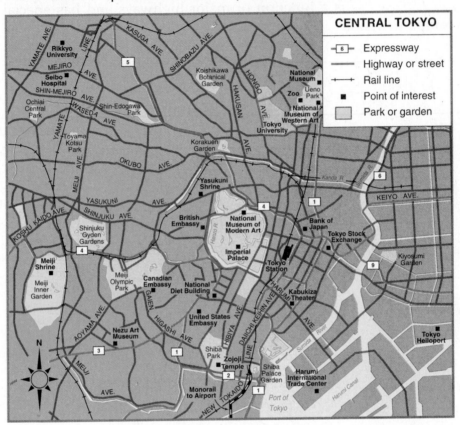

1. Based on the map, what are two physical and two human features of Tokyo?

_____

_____

2. Name a human feature that is in Tokyo because Tokyo is the national capital.

_____

3. How do the features of Tokyo differ from those in your town or city?

_____

_____

_____

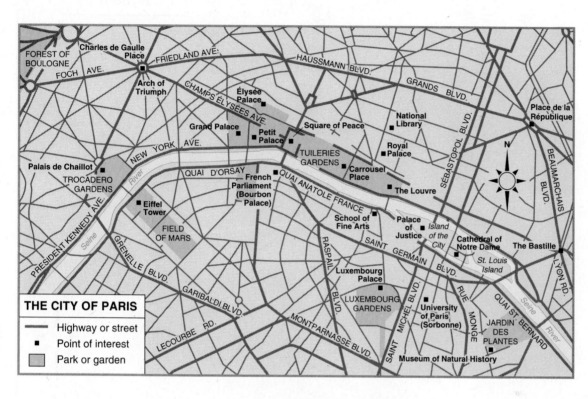

THE CITY OF PARIS

— Highway or street
■ Point of interest
▨ Park or garden

4. Based on the map, name a physical feature of Paris.

_____

5. Name three human features of Paris other than buildings.

_____

_____

6. How do the features of Paris differ from those of Tokyo?

_____

_____

_____

7. What are two famous buildings in Paris shown on the map?

_____

_____

5 Relief and Elevation

By reading a **relief map** you can learn something about the physical features of a place. The map on this page is a relief map of Russia. Russia is now an independent country. It was formerly part of the Union of Soviet Socialist Republics.

Shading on relief maps shows the shape and height of the land. The highest, steepest mountain ranges have dark shading. Lower, less steep mountain ranges have lighter shading. Valleys and plains have no shading.

Besides mountains, relief maps usually show the major rivers of a place. A river's **source** is where it begins. A river flows downhill towards its **mouth**, where it empties into a sea or ocean. Many rivers flow into other rivers. These smaller rivers are called **tributaries**.

► Name a tributary of the Lena River.

► Name three rivers that flow north.

► Does the Ob River flow mainly through low lands or high lands?

► In which mountain range are the sources of the Ural and Volga Rivers? These rivers empty into what sea?

► What is the longest mountain range in Russia?

► What other landforms are shown on this map?

► What other water forms are shown on this map?

► What mountain on this map is 10,325 feet high?

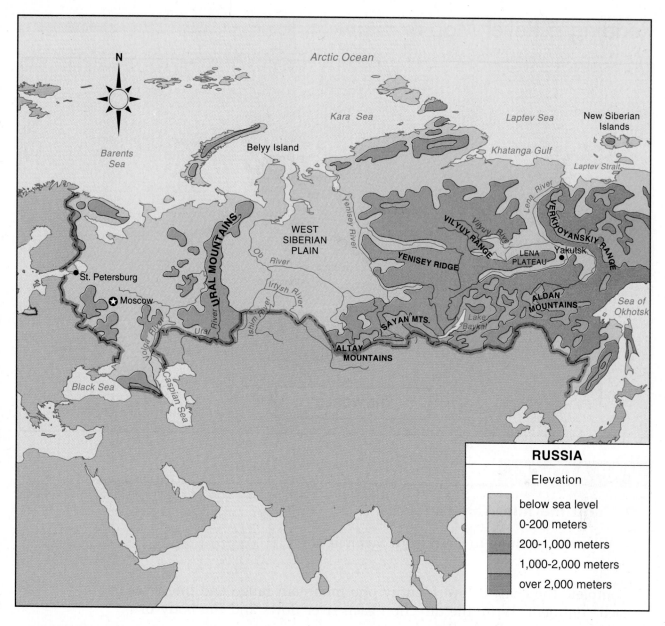

This map shows part of Russia. Colors on the map show how high the land is, or its elevation. **Elevation** is the height of the land above or below the level of the sea. Read the legend to understand what elevation each color represents.

► What color shows the highest areas in Russia?

► What color shows the lowest areas?

Like a relief map, an elevation map gives a picture of how the land looks. An elevation map uses zones of color to show areas of land with similar elevation. A relief map gives an almost three-dimensional picture of the land. In what ways might we use relief and elevation maps?

► These places are in which elevation zones?

      Moscow   Lake Baykal   Yakutsk

► At what elevation is the source of the Ural River?

► Where in Russia is the elevation lowest?

Reading a Relief Map

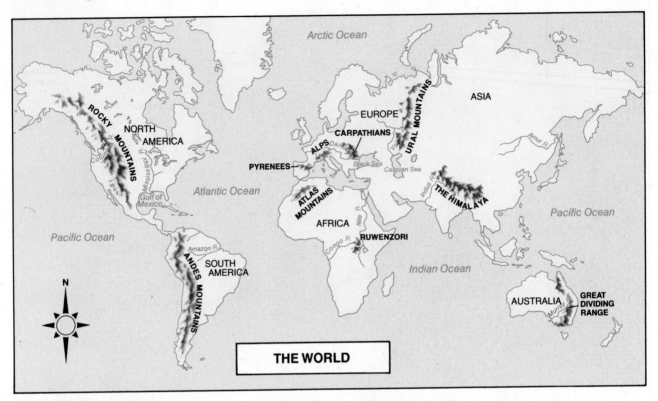

THE WORLD

MAP ATTACK!

- **Read the title.** This map shows _____.

  What is one thing to learn from this map? _____

1. Complete the chart below. Identify one mountain range and one river in each continent. Write the direction each river flows and the body of water into which it empties.

Continent	Mountain Range	River	Direction	Body of Water
a. North America	_____	_____	_____	_____
b. South America	_____	_____	_____	_____
c. Asia	_____	_____	_____	_____
d. Europe	_____	_____	_____	_____
e. Australia	_____	_____	_____	_____

2. Draw a conclusion. Rivers may flow north, south, east, or west. What determines the direction that a river flows?

_____

Reading an Elevation Map

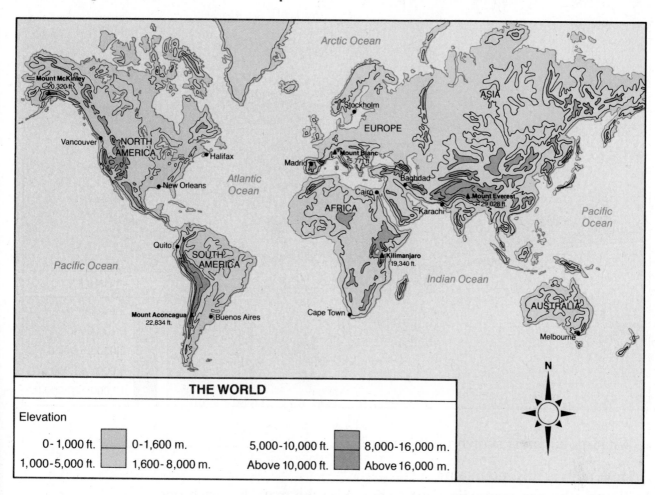

THE WORLD

Elevation

0-1,000 ft.	0-1,600 m.	5,000-10,000 ft.	8,000-16,000 m.
1,000-5,000 ft.	1,600-8,000 m.	Above 10,000 ft.	Above 16,000 m.

N

1. Circle the places in this list that are between 0 and 1,000 feet above sea level.

   New Orleans   Baghdad   Madrid   Cairo   Cape Town

   Karachi   Stockholm   Buenos Aires   Melbourne

2. Write the elevation and continent of these mountain peaks.

Mountain	Elevation	Continent
a. Aconcagua	_____	_____
b. Blanc	_____	_____
c. Everest	_____	_____
d. McKinley	_____	_____
e. Kilimanjaro	_____	_____

3. Draw a conclusion. The largest area of land more than 10,000 feet above

   sea level is on which continent? _____

Reading a Map of Turkey

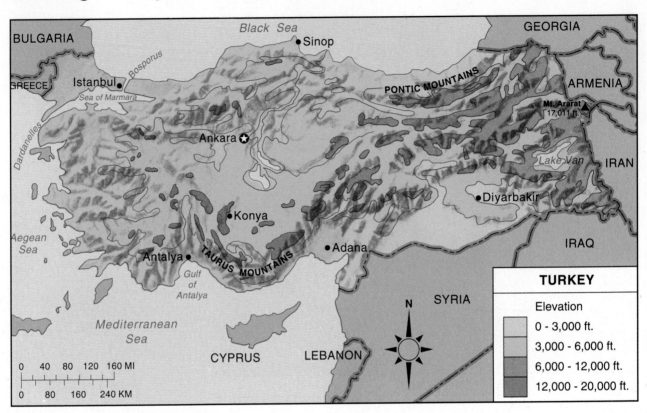

1. What mountain is shown on this map? _____

   How high is this mountain? _____
2. Identify the two mountain ranges shown on the map. For each one, identify the part of the country in which it is located.

   <u>Mountain Range</u>   <u>Part of Country</u>

   a. _____   _____

   b. _____   _____

3. Is the eastern or western part of Turkey more mountainous? _____
4. Does the elevation of the land increase or decrease as it approaches the

   coast? _____

5. About how far from Istanbul is Mt. Ararat? _____

6. About how far from Sinop is Adana? _____
7. Imagine you are traveling by boat from Antalya in southern Turkey to Sinop in northern Turkey. List the bodies of water you must cross.

   _____

   _____

Skill Check

Vocabulary Check   relief   elevation   mouth

                                         tributaries   source

Write the word that best completes each sentence.

1. A(n) _____ map uses shading to show mountains on a map.

2. A(n) _____ map uses zones of color to show the height of land.

3. A river's _____ is where it begins, and its _____ is where it empties into a sea or ocean.

4. Rivers that flow into a larger river are _____.

Map Check

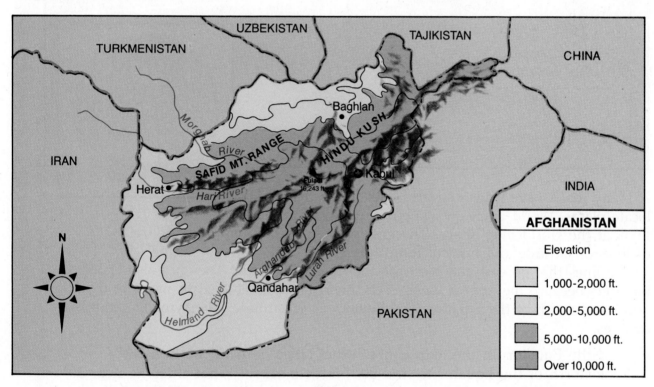

1. Name two tributaries of the Helmand River.

   _____

2. Name a river that flows through the Safid Mt. Range.

   _____

3. Name a river whose source is in the Hindu Kush Mountains.

   _____

4. Where are the areas of lowest elevation in Afghanistan?

   _____

6 Latitude and Longitude

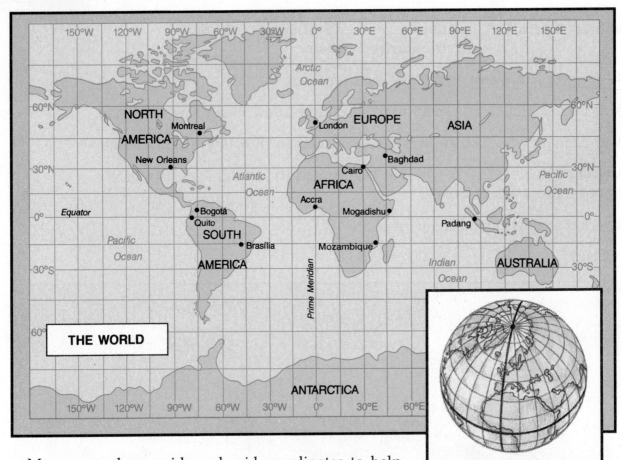

Many maps have grids and grid coordinates to help locate places. World maps and globes have grids on them. Look at the world map above. The grid pattern on the map is made up of lines of **latitude** and lines of **longitude**.

The lines that go east and west are the lines of latitude. They are also called **parallels** because they never touch each other. Latitude is used to measure distances north and south of the Equator. The Equator is 0° latitude. The symbol ° stands for **degrees**.

▶ Find the Equator on the map above. What cities lie near the Equator? Look north of the Equator to find 30° North latitude. What cities lie near 30° North latitude? Find 15° South latitude. What cities lie near 15° South latitude?

The lines that go north and south are the lines of longitude. They are also called **meridians**. Longitude is used to measure distances east and west of the **Prime Meridian**. The Prime Meridian is 0° longitude and goes from the North Pole to the South Pole. All lines of longitude meet at the North and South Poles.

▶ Find the Prime Meridian at 0° longitude. What cities lie near the Prime Meridian? Now look east of the Prime Meridian to find 45° East longitude. What cities lie near 45° East longitude? Find 75° West longitude. What cities lie near 75° West longitude?

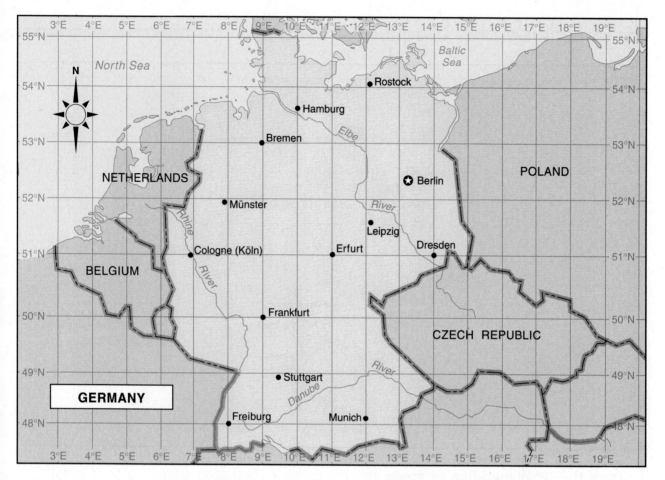

Look at the map of the world on page 42. You can see that the lines of latitude begin with 0° at the Equator and increase as they go north and south. The highest numbers are at the poles. The North Pole is 90° North latitude, and the South Pole is 90° South latitude.

The lines of longitude begin with 0° at the Prime Meridian and increase as they go east and west of the Prime Meridian. The highest number is 180°. The line of longitude directly opposite the Prime Meridian is 180°.

The lines of latitude and longitude form a grid pattern. This grid enables us to locate every place on Earth. Look at the map above. Find 51° North latitude. Run your finger along it until it crosses 7° East longitude. You have found the city of Cologne. The coordinates of Cologne are 51° North latitude and 7° East longitude, or 51°N, 7°E. Every spot on Earth has its own coordinates.

► Use latitude and longitude coordinates to find these places on the map. The coordinate for latitude is always named first.

Frankfurt	50°N, 9°E
Bremen	53°N, 9°E
Munich	48°N, 12°E

► Estimate the coordinates (latitude and longitude) of these places on the map:

Münster
Leipzig
Stuttgart

Using Latitude and Longitude

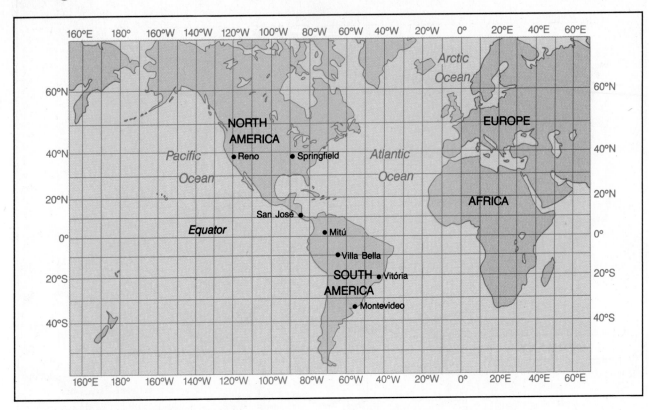

1. Trace the 70° W meridian in green.

   a. Is that line east or west of the Prime Meridian? _____

   b. Is most of the area shown on the map in the Eastern or Western

   Hemisphere? _____

2. Trace the Equator in red.
   Draw an N just north of the Equator.
   Draw an S just south of the Equator.

3. a. What city is near the place where the Equator and 70°W cross?

   _____

   b. What are its coordinates? _____, 70°W.

4. Find the missing coordinate for these cities.

   a. Springfield   40°N   , _____

   b. Vitória   _____,   40°W

   c. Reno   _____,   120°W

   d. San José   10°N   , _____

   e. Villa Bella   _____,   65°W

   f. Montevideo   35°S   , _____

Using Latitude and Longitude

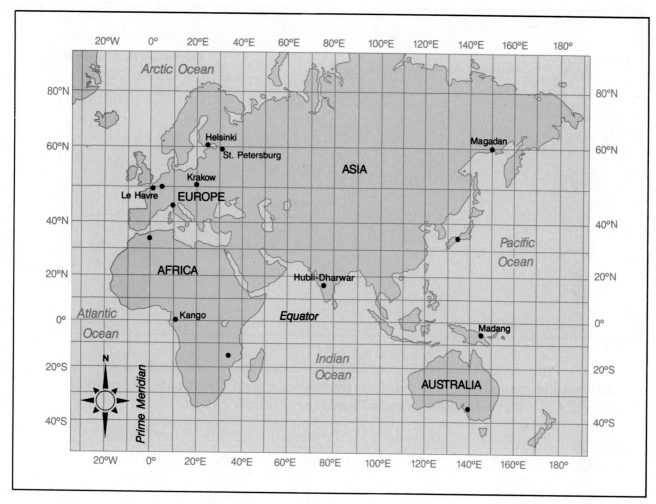

1. Label the cities at these locations on the map.
   a. 35° S, 140°E   Murray Bridge
   b. 50°N,   5°E   Namur
   c. 35°N, 135°E   Osaka
   d. 45°N,   10°E   Parma
   e. 15° S,   35°E   Zomba
   f. 35°N,   0°   Saida

2. Write the latitude and longitude coordinates of these cities.

	Latitude	Longitude
a. Helsinki	_____	_____
b. Le Havre	_____	_____
c. St. Petersburg	_____	_____
d. Madang	_____	_____
e. Krakow	_____	_____
f. Hubli-Dharwar	_____	_____

Tracking a Hurricane

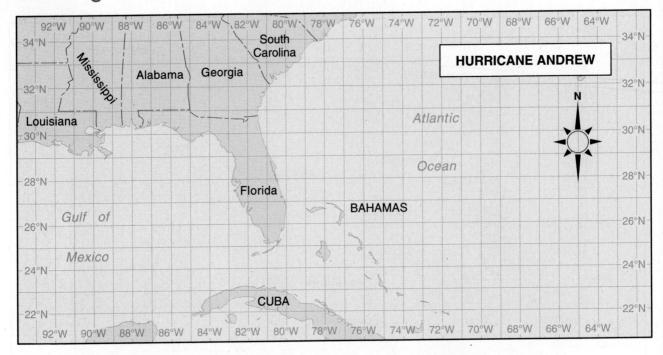

1. Use the latitude and longitude coordinates to track Hurricane Andrew's path on the map above. Put a dot on the map for each coordinate. Number each dot. Connect the dots to track Hurricane Andrew's path.

Position	Latitude	Longitude	Position	Latitude	Longitude
1	24°N	63°W	9	26°N	85°W
2	25°N	65°W	10	26½°N	87°W
3	26°N	69°W	11	27½°N	89°W
4	25½°N	72°W	12	29°N	91°W
5	25½°N	74°W	13	30°N	91½°W
6	25½°N	76½°W	14	31°N	91½°W
7	25½°N	79°W	15	31½°N	91°W
8	25½°N	81°W	16	32°N	90°W

2. Write the direction that Hurricane Andrew traveled

   a. from Position 1 to Position 3. _____

   b. from Position 4 to Position 8. _____

   c. from Position 9 to Position 13. _____

   d. from Position 14 to Position 16. _____

3. In what body of water did the hurricane begin? _____

4. What other body of water did it cross? _____

5. Where did Hurricane Andrew hit land?

   _____

Skill Check

Vocabulary Check   latitude   degrees   longitude
                         meridians   parallels   Prime Meridian

Write the word or phrase that best completes each sentence.

1. The _____ is the starting point for measuring distances east and west.

2. Lines of latitude, also called _____, measure distances north and south of the Equator.

3. Lines of longitude, also called _____, meet at the poles.

Map Check

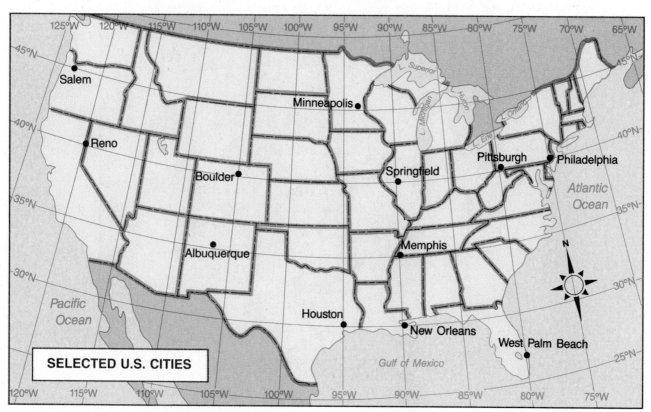

SELECTED U.S. CITIES

1. Name the cities at these locations.

    a. 40°N, 90°W _____   c. 40°N, 105°W _____

    b. 40°N, 75°W _____   d. 35°N, 90°W _____

2. Write the latitude and longitude coordinates of these cities.

	Latitude	Longitude			Latitude	Longitude
a. New Orleans				c. Reno		
b. Pittsburgh				d. Houston		

Geography Themes Up Close

Location describes where a place is found. Every place on Earth has a location. There are two ways to describe location. **Relative location** describes a place by what it is near or what is around it. **Absolute location** is the specific address or latitude and longitude coordinates of a place. For example, the postal address of your home is an absolute location.

1. Venezuela is in the northern part of South America. This country is located along the Caribbean Sea. Label Venezuela on the map.

2. This South American country is found in the central part of the continent. It is southeast of Peru and north of Argentina. Write the name of the country here and then label it on the map.

_____

3. Label these national capitals on the map.
   a. Lima 12°S, 77°W
   b. Cayenne 5°N, 52°W

4. Mount Aconcagua's absolute location is 33°S, 70°W. Circle Mount Aconcagua on the map.

5. Name the cities found at these locations:
   a. 5°N, 75°W _____   c. 26°S, 58°W_____

   b. 19°S, 65°W _____   d. 6°N, 55°W _____

6. Find the Amazon River. Describe its relative location.

_____

_____

_____

7. What is the absolute location of the Mato Grosso Plateau?

_____

8. Name the country located at 33°S, 55°W.

_____

9. Give the absolute location of Brasília, Brazil.

_____

10. Describe the relative location of the country of Guyana.

_____

_____

_____

7 Climate Maps

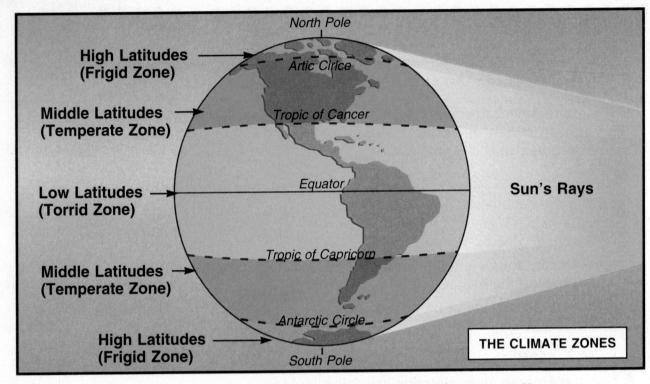

High Latitudes (Frigid Zone)

Middle Latitudes (Temperate Zone)

Low Latitudes (Torrid Zone)

Middle Latitudes (Temperate Zone)

High Latitudes (Frigid Zone)

North Pole
Artic Cirlce
Tropic of Cancer
Equator
Tropic of Capricorn
Antarctic Circle
South Pole

Sun's Rays

THE CLIMATE ZONES

Climate is the weather of an area over a long period of time. Many different factors determine what kind of climate a place has. Some factors include elevation, winds, and whether the place is near water.

One of the most important factors in determining climate is how directly the rays of the sun hit the place. Because Earth is round, the sun's rays do not hit it evenly. In places near the Equator, the sun is directly overhead. These places receive direct rays. In places near the poles, the sun is low in the sky. These places receive slanted rays. The direct rays give more heat. The slanted rays give less heat.

The world can be divided into **climate zones** based on how directly the sun's rays strike Earth. Look at the map above to find the climate zones.

The **low latitudes**, or **Torrid Zone**, is the area between the Tropic of Cancer (23½°N) and the Tropic of Capricorn (23½°S). *Torrid* means "very hot." The sun's direct rays heat the Torrid Zone all year round.

The **high latitudes**, or **Frigid Zones**, cover the area between the Arctic Circle (66½°N) and the North Pole (90°N) and the area between the Antarctic Circle (66½°S) and the South Pole (90°S). *Frigid* means "very cold." The sun is low in the sky in these areas, so only slanted rays hit them. As a result, these zones are cold all year.

The **middle latitudes**, or **Temperate Zones**, are between the Torrid Zone and the Frigid Zones. *Temperate* means "balanced." The climate in the Temperate Zones is a balance between the heat of the Torrid Zone and the cold of the Frigid Zones. The climate of places in the Temperate Zones changes from season to season.

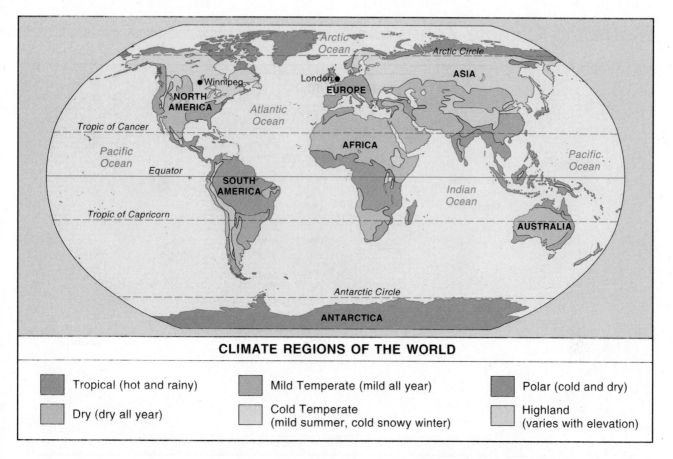

CLIMATE REGIONS OF THE WORLD

- Tropical (hot and rainy)
- Dry (dry all year)
- Mild Temperate (mild all year)
- Cold Temperate (mild summer, cold snowy winter)
- Polar (cold and dry)
- Highland (varies with elevation)

Not all places within a climate zone have the same climate. For example, Winnipeg, Canada, and London, England, are both in the Temperate Zone. The rays of sunlight that strike Winnipeg are about as direct as the ones that strike London. Yet the two places have very different climates. London has a much warmer climate because it is near the sea. This is an example of how factors other than sunlight affect the climate of a place.

To reflect differences within climate zones, a list of **climate regions** has been developed. There are six basic climate regions. As you read about the climate regions of the world, locate them on the map above.

The **tropical climate** is hot and rainy. Much of the world's rain forests and jungles grow in tropical climates.

Areas that have a **dry climate** are dry all year round. Much of the western United States has a dry climate. So does northern Africa, where the great Sahara desert is.

The **mild temperate climate** is mild all year.

Areas with **cold temperate climates** have mild summers, but the winters are cold and snowy.

Areas with a **polar climate** are cold and dry.

► Find the polar climates on the map. Why do you think this climate has the name it does?

Mountainous areas have a **highland climate**, which varies with the elevation.

Every place on Earth has one of these six climate regions. Find where you live on the map. In which climate region do you live?

Mastering Climate Zones

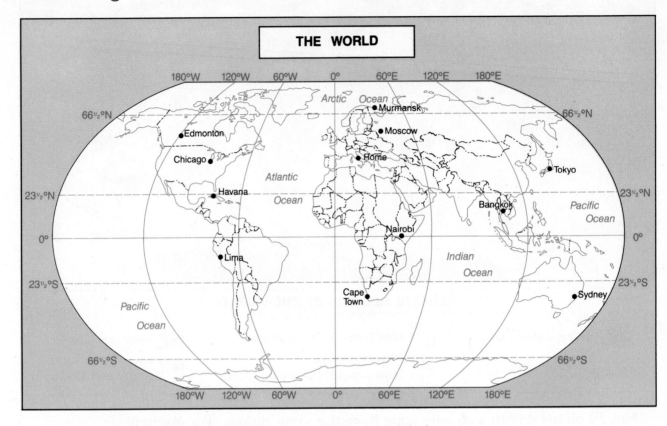

1. Label the following places on the map. Write two labels twice.

   Equator   Tropic of Cancer   Arctic Circle   Frigid Zone
   Antarctic Circle Tropic of Capricorn   Torrid Zone   Temperate Zone

2. Lightly color the Torrid Zone orange, the Temperate Zones yellow, and the Frigid Zones blue.

3. After each city below, write its climate zone. Then write whether it is in the high, middle, or low latitudes.

Place	Climate Zone	Latitudes
a. Murmansk	_____	_____
b. Chicago	_____	_____
c. Cape Town	_____	_____
d. Nairobi	_____	_____
e. Tokyo	_____	_____
f. Havana	_____	_____
g. Rome	_____	_____
h. Bangkok	_____	_____
i. Lima	_____	_____

Reading a Climate Map

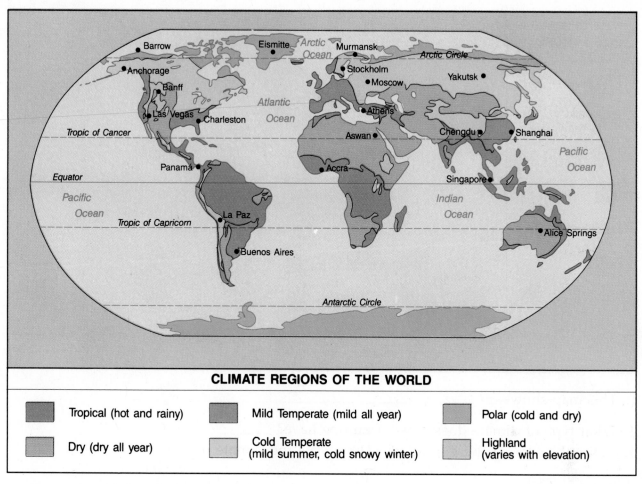

CLIMATE REGIONS OF THE WORLD

■ Tropical (hot and rainy)	■ Mild Temperate (mild all year)	■ Polar (cold and dry)
■ Dry (dry all year)	■ Cold Temperate (mild summer, cold snowy winter)	■ Highland (varies with elevation)

This map shows six climate regions of the world.

Write the name of three cities in each climate region.

1. Tropical _____ _____ _____

2. Dry _____ _____ _____

3. Mild Temperate _____ _____ _____

4. Cold Temperate _____ _____ _____

5. Polar _____ _____ _____

6. Highland _____ _____ _____

7. Which climate is found mostly in the Frigid Zone? _____

8. The tropical region is found mostly in what climate zone? _____

9. Draw a conclusion. Which has the most areas with cold snowy winters, the Northern or the Southern Hemisphere?

_____

Reading a Climate Map of Europe

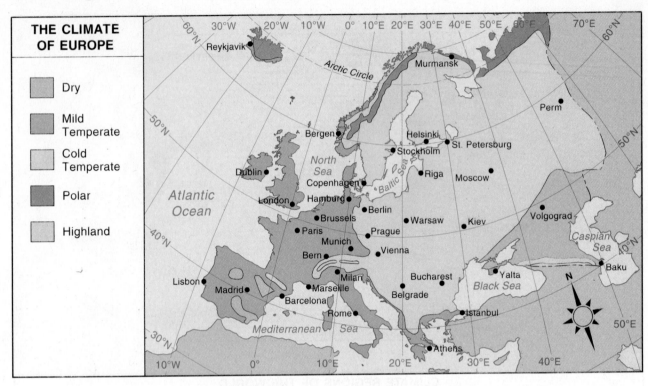

THE CLIMATE
OF EUROPE

- Dry
- Mild Temperate
- Cold Temperate
- Polar
- Highland

1. This map shows _____

2. What type of climate does most of Europe have? _____

3. Name the cities at these locations. Then write the climate region.

   a. 60°N, 25°E   _____   _____

   b. 50°N, 45°E   _____   _____

   c. 60°N, 5°E   _____   _____

   d. 45°N, 20°E   _____   _____

   e. 55°N, 5°W   _____   _____

4. Estimate the degrees latitude and longitude of each city. Then write its climate region.

	Latitude	Longitude	Climate Region
a. St. Petersburg			
b. Kiev			
c. London			
d. Baku			
e. Madrid			

5. Polar regions on this map do not extend below what line of latitude? _____

✓ Skill Check

Vocabulary Check Torrid Zone   high latitudes   climate
Temperate Zone   middle latitudes
Frigid Zone   low latitudes

Write the word or phrase that best completes each sentence.

1. The Temperate Zone is found in the _____.
2. The area between the Tropic of Cancer and the Tropic of Capricorn

   is called the _____ , or _____ .

3. The high latitudes are also called the _____.

4. The weather of an area over a long period of time is its _____ .

Map Check

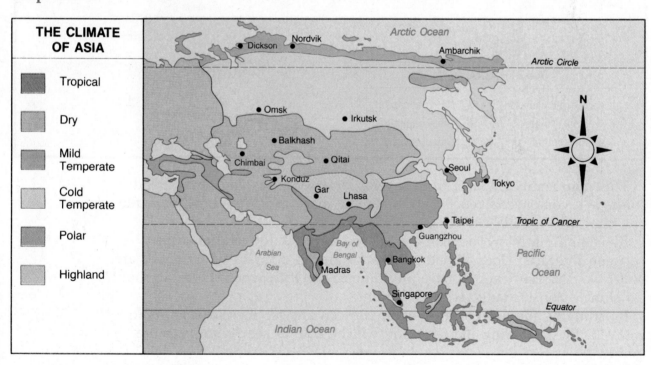

1. Write the names of three cities in each climate region.

   a. Tropical   _____   _____   _____

   b. Dry   _____   _____   _____

   c. Mild Temperate _____   _____   _____

   d. Cold Temperate _____   _____   _____

   e. Polar   _____   _____   _____

   f. Highland   _____   _____   _____

Combining Maps

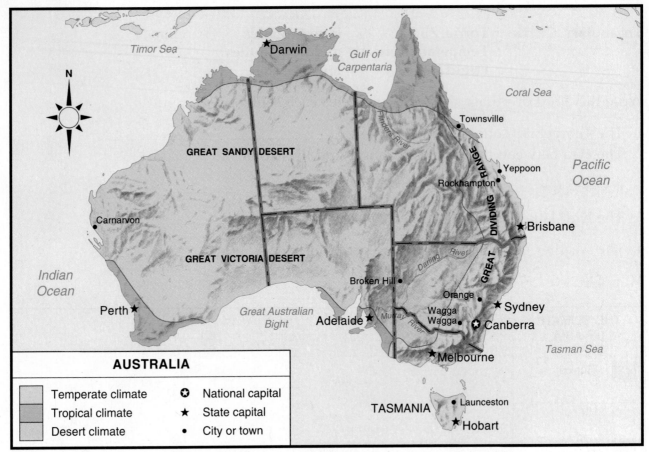

This map combines facts from several kinds of maps you have already studied. It combines a relief map, a climate map, and a political map into one map of Australia.

By combining many facts on a map, we can look for **relationships** between the facts. Does climate have anything to do with where cities are built? Do physical features have anything to do with where cities are built? Do climate zones change with elevation?

By studying the facts on this map, you can answer these questions for yourself. By comparing the facts you will be able to see Australia more clearly.

Read the Facts

► What and where are the seas, gulfs, and oceans that surround Australia?

► What and where are Australia's main mountain range and deserts?

► Where are Australia's temperate, tropical, and desert climates?

Draw Conclusions

► In what climate zone are most of Australia's cities?

► Near what physical features are most of Australia's cities?

► Where in Australia do very few people live?
Why do few people live there?

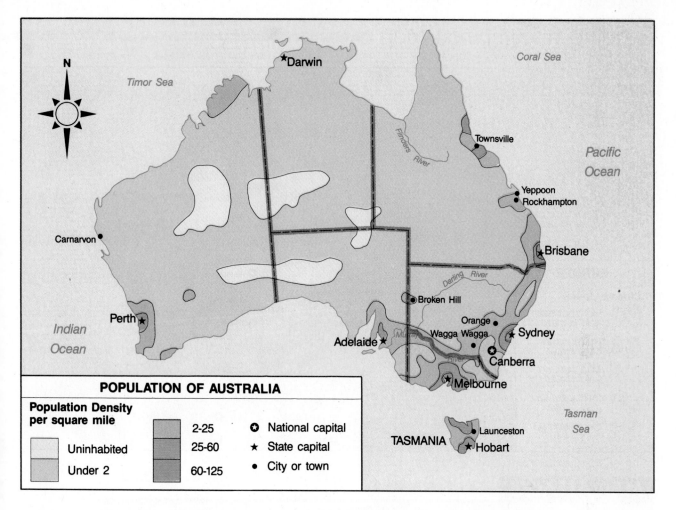

POPULATION OF AUSTRALIA

Population Density per square mile

Uninhabited	2-25
Under 2	25-60
	60-125

○ National capital
★ State capital
• City or town

The map on this page shows Australia's population density. **Population density** is how many people live in a square mile. Parts of Australia are uninhabited, no one lives there. The darkest colors on the map stand for the places with the densest (most crowded) population. Find the area around Sydney, Australia's biggest city.

Read the key to learn what the purple color stands for. Closest to Sydney there are between 60 and 125 people living in each square mile. Point to Sydney, then move your finger inland (west or northwest). As you move away from the main part of the city, the population becomes less and less dense.

Read the Facts

► What are the five most densely populated places in Australia?

Compare the Maps Compare the facts on the map on this page and the map on page 56 to answer the questions.

► What is the population density in Australia's desert regions?

► What is the population density in the mountain region?

► What is the population density in the regions with mild temperate climates?

Draw a Conclusion

► On the whole, which climate does Australia's population prefer?

Reading a Combined Map

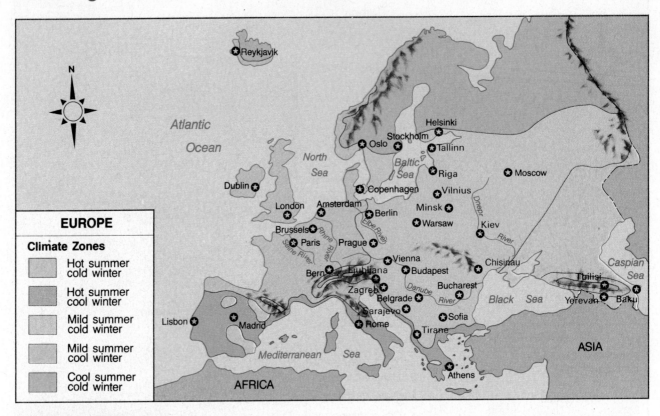

EUROPE

Climate Zones

- Hot summer cold winter
- Hot summer cool winter
- Mild summer cold winter
- Mild summer cool winter
- Cool summer cold winter

MAP ATTACK!

- **Read the title.** This map shows _____.
- **Read the compass rose.** Label the intermediate direction arrows.

1. What information is combined on this map?

   _____

2. Name one major water form near each of these climate zones.

   a. mild summer, cold winter _____

   b. hot summer, cold winter _____

   c. mild summer, cool winter _____

3. Name two cities in each of these climate zones.

   a. hot summer, cool winter _____

   b. mild summer, cool winter _____

   c. mild summer, cold winter _____

4. Find the Danube River. Name the capital cities that are along the

   Danube River. _____

Reading a Combined Map

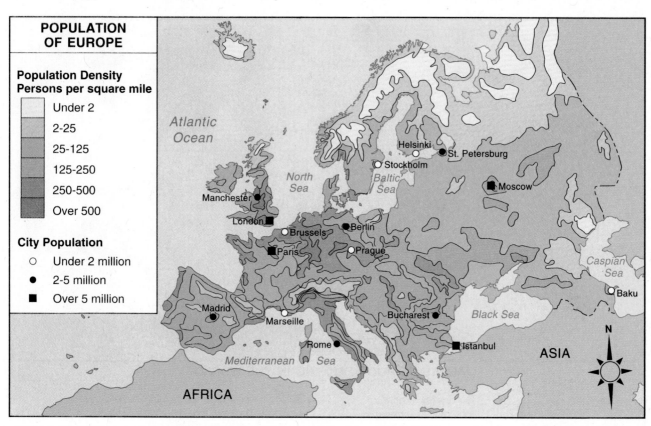

POPULATION OF EUROPE

Population Density
Persons per square mile

- Under 2
- 2-25
- 25-125
- 125-250
- 250-500
- Over 500

City Population
- ○ Under 2 million
- ● 2-5 million
- ■ Over 5 million

1. Name four cities that have more than 5 million people.

   _____

2. Name six cities that have 2 to 5 million people.

   _____

   _____

3. Name six cities that have less than 2 million people.

   _____

   _____

4. Is the population density higher or lower around the cities? _____

   Why do you think this is so? _____

5. What is the population density of most of the areas around the Baltic

   Sea? _____

6. Draw a conclusion. Look at the map on page 58. What climate zone has

   the lowest population density? _____

   Why do you think this is so? _____

Reading a Combined Map

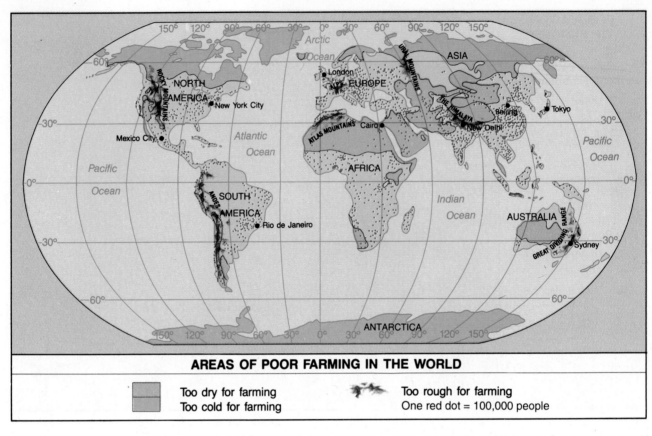

AREAS OF POOR FARMING IN THE WORLD

Too dry for farming	Too rough for farming
Too cold for farming	One red dot = 100,000 people

1. What two continents have the largest area of land too dry for farming?

   _____

2. What continent is completely without a settled population?

   _____

3. What continent is too cold for farming? _____

4. What continent has the most areas of dense population? _____

5. Label the following places on the map.

   <u>Sahara Desert</u> an area in northern Africa too dry for farming
   <u>Gobi Desert</u> an area north of the Himalaya too dry for farming
   <u>Kalahari Desert</u> an area in southern Africa too dry for farming
   <u>Great Victoria Desert</u> an area in western Australia too dry for farming

6. Draw a conclusion. Name three conditions that make land poor for farming. Then name one place in the world that fits each condition.

Condition	Place
_____	_____
_____	_____
_____	_____

Skill Check

Vocabulary Check   **relationships**   **population density**

Write the word or phrase that best completes the sentence.

1. The number of people per square mile is _____.

2. You can find _____ when you combine or compare facts.

Map Check

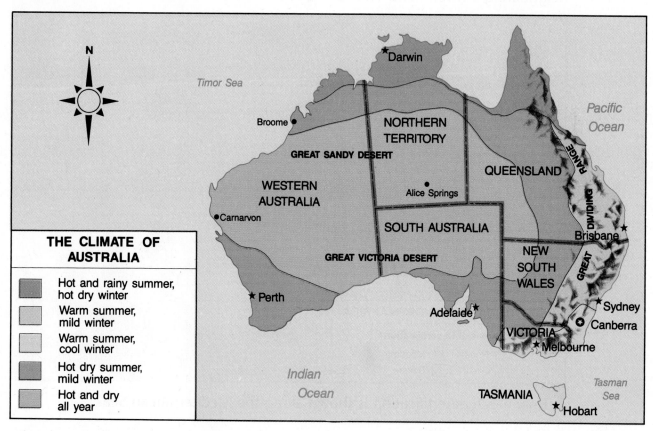

1. What is the climate of these cities?

   a. Sydney _____

   b. Darwin _____

   c. Alice Springs _____

   d. Perth _____

2. What is the climate of Tasmania? _____

3. How is the climate east of the Great Dividing Range different from

   the climate west of it? _____

4. Which state has the least variety in climate? _____

Geography Themes Up Close

Human/Environment Interaction describes how people change or adapt to the environment. Some changes to the land cause problems. In North Africa, much of the land is desert. In what ways would a desert environment affect the people who live there? In some areas of North Africa, **desertification** has become a problem. Desertification is the spread of desert conditions into the neighboring environment. This results in an increase in the size of the desert.

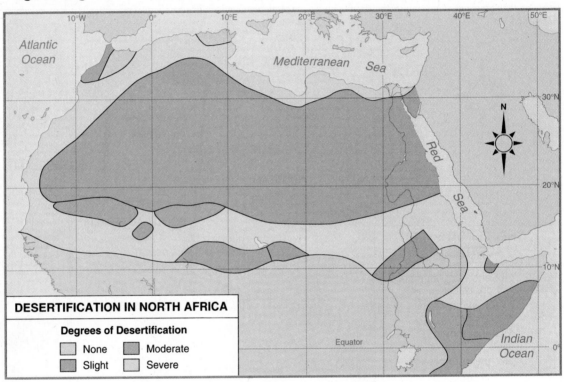

DESERTIFICATION IN NORTH AFRICA

Degrees of Desertification

- None
- Slight
- Moderate
- Severe

1. How much desertification is shown along the Mediterranean Sea?

   _____

2. Describe the desertification between 10°N and 20°N latitudes.

   _____

   _____

3. Explain why it would be helpful for geographers to know the locations, kinds, and causes of desertification in North Africa.

   _____

   _____

   _____

For hundreds of years, the Dutch people of the Netherlands have worked to **reclaim,** or take back, land that has been flooded. They built dikes around the flooded areas and drained the water. The Dutch call this reclaimed land "polders."

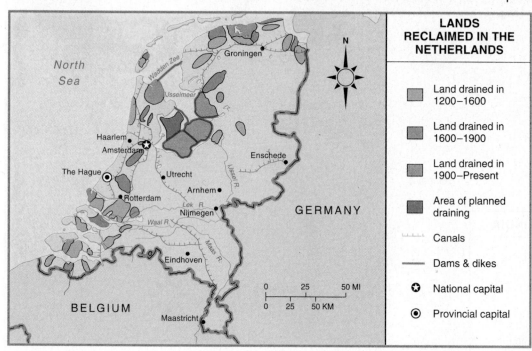

LANDS RECLAIMED IN THE NETHERLANDS

- Land drained in 1200–1600
- Land drained in 1600–1900
- Land drained in 1900–Present
- Area of planned draining
- Canals
- Dams & dikes
- ⭐ National capital
- ◉ Provincial capital

4. During which time period did the Dutch reclaim the most land?

_____

5. Along which bodies of water was land reclaimed?

_____

6. What are the locations of future polders?

_____

7. Based on the map, how have the Dutch worked with their environment besides building polders, dams, and dikes?

_____

8. How would you judge the interaction of the Dutch with their environment? How has it been beneficial or harmful? Explain.

_____

_____

Comparing Maps

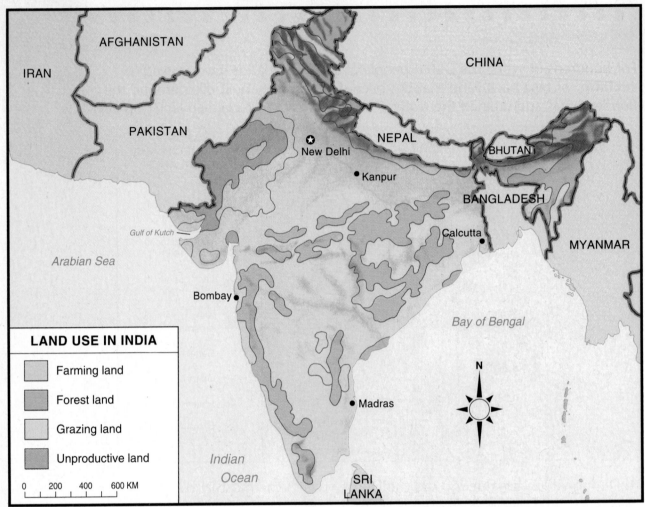

LAND USE IN INDIA

- Farming land
- Forest land
- Grazing land
- Unproductive land

0   200   400   600 KM

Comparing two maps of the same place can help you to get a better understanding of that place. The map on this page shows how land is used in India. The map on page 65 shows the products that are grown or mined in each region of India. Before you begin comparing the maps, use your **Map Attack!** skills to become familiar with each map.

- **Read the title.** What can you expect to learn from each map?
- **Read the legend.** Find an example of each land use on this map. Find an example of each resource on the next map.
- **Read the compass rose.** Find north on each map.
- **Read the scale.** Are distances measured in miles or kilometers? Is the scale the same on both maps?

After you are familiar with each map, study each map separately to see what you can learn. Read the facts on each map.

► India's unproductive land is mostly in which region?

► India's northeast region is mostly used for what?

► What is the most widespread land use in India?

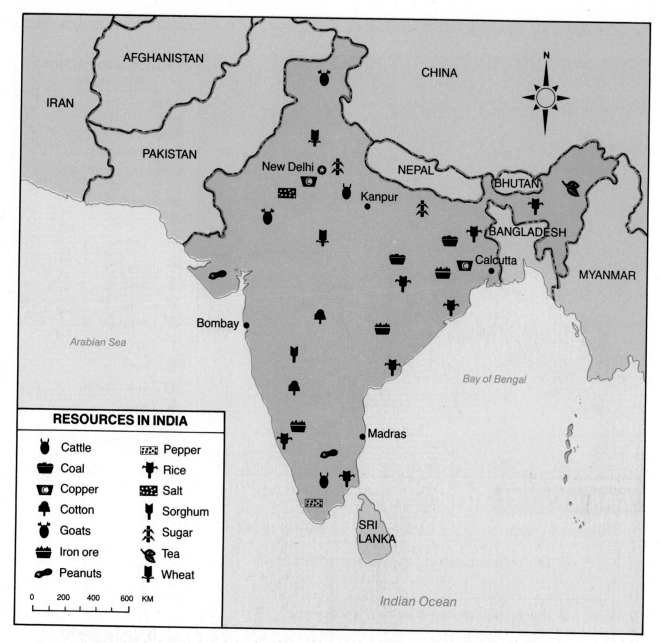

RESOURCES IN INDIA

Cattle		Pepper	
Coal		Rice	
Copper		Salt	
Cotton		Sorghum	
Goats		Sugar	
Iron ore		Tea	
Peanuts		Wheat	

0 200 400 600 KM

Once you are familiar with each map, you can begin comparing them. To compare land use and resources in the southern tip of India, first find the southern tip of India on each map. Make sure you are looking at the same area of India on each map. Is the pepper from southern India found in forest or farm land?

Now compare other areas of India. Use the legend of each map to help you answer these questions.

► What is the land use in most coal-mining areas of India?

► What is the land use in the area where goats are a product?

► What is the land use where salt is mined?

► What is the land use around each of these manufacturing centers?

      Calcutta   Bombay   Madras   New Delhi

► What resources are found near those manufacturing centers?

Comparing Maps

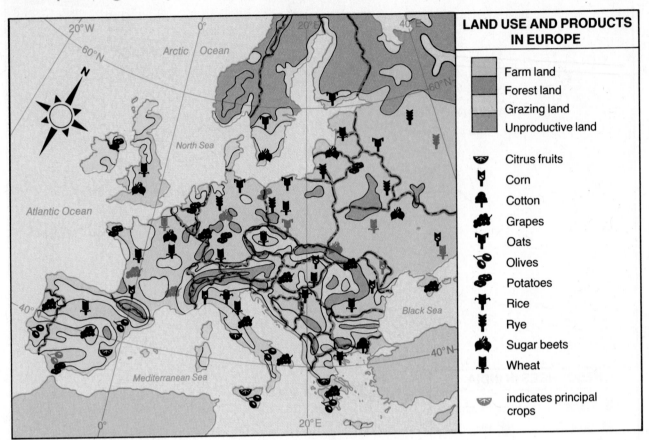

LAND USE AND PRODUCTS IN EUROPE

Farm land
Forest land
Grazing land
Unproductive land

Citrus fruits
Corn
Cotton
Grapes
Oats
Olives
Potatoes
Rice
Rye
Sugar beets
Wheat

indicates principal crops

MAP ATTACK!

Follow the steps on page 64 to begin reading this map.

1. What are the principal crops in southern Europe?

_____

2. What are the principal crops in eastern Europe?

_____

3. What is the main land use in Europe north of 60°N?

_____

4. Where are Europe's largest forests? _____

5. What is the main land use north of the Black Sea?

_____

6. Circle the crops most often grown where grapes are grown.

     rye   cotton   oats   olives   citrus fruits   corn   wheat

7. Circle the crops most often grown where wheat is grown.

     sugar beets   rye   oats   cotton   potatoes   olives   grapes

Comparing Maps

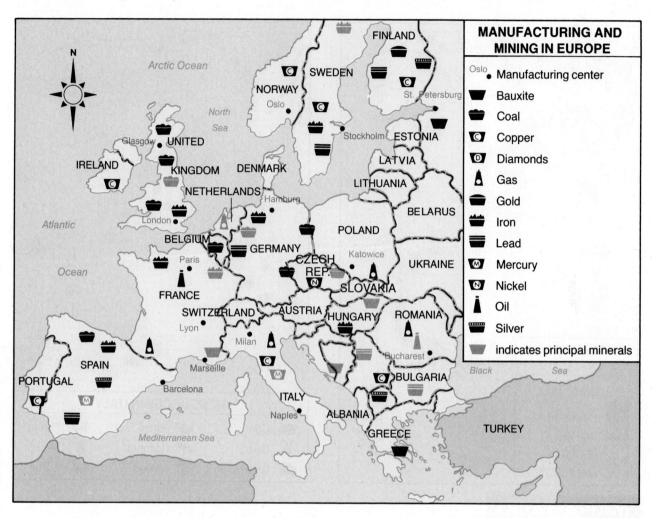

MANUFACTURING AND MINING IN EUROPE

- • Manufacturing center
- Bauxite
- Coal
- Copper
- Diamonds
- Gas
- Gold
- Iron
- Lead
- Mercury
- Nickel
- Oil
- Silver
- indicates principal minerals

1. Name five manufacturing centers in southern Europe.

_____

2. Name five manufacturing centers in northern Europe.

_____

3. Circle the principal crops and minerals in each of these countries.

   a. France   bauxite   grapes   gold   wheat   iron

   b. Spain   oats   olives   mercury   grapes   gas

   c. Italy   copper   rice   oil   corn   mercury

4. List the mining and farming industries in each of these countries.

   a. Greece   _____

   b. Italy   _____

   c. Hungary _____

Comparing Maps

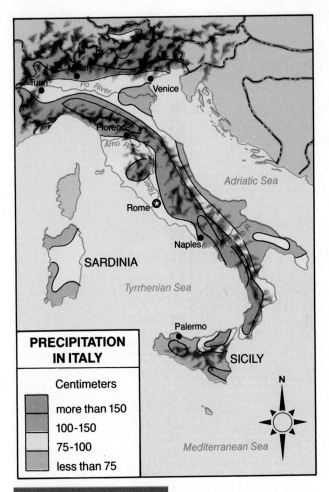

PRECIPITATION IN ITALY

Centimeters

	more than 150
	100-150
	75-100
	less than 75

RESOURCES IN ITALY

	Coal		Hogs		Poultry
	Goats		Lumber		Sheep
	Grapes		Olives		Sulfur

MAP ATTACK!

Follow the steps on page 64 to compare the maps.

1. Circle the resources that are found near each city.

    a. Rome   olives   lumber   hogs   sheep   coal

    b. Florence   goats   olives   sheep   grapes   hogs

    c. Turin   sheep   coal   grapes   poultry   olives

2. Name three resources found along the Po River.

    _____

3. Name three resources found mostly in the northern mountains.

    _____

4. Name two resources found mostly in drier areas. _____

5. Name three resources found in the rainy area of northern Italy.

    _____

✓ Skill Check

Vocabulary Check   comparing

Circle the best ending for the following sentence.

Comparing two different maps of the same place is

  a. necessary for you to determine directions.

  b. a good way to help you understand the place.

  c. the only way to learn about a country's products.

Map Check

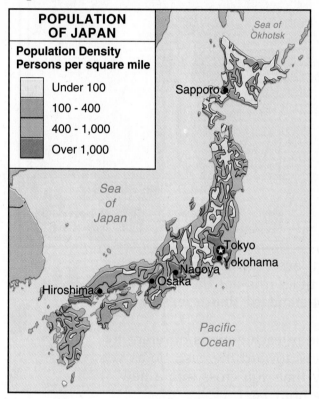

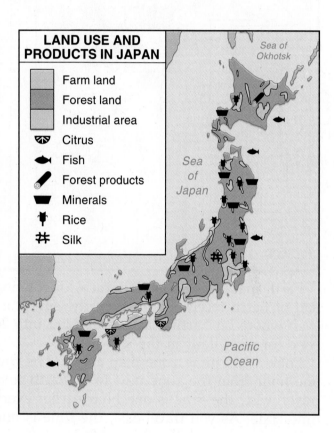

1. a. The map on the left shows _____.

  b. The map on the right shows _____.

2. Is the population density of Japan higher along the coasts or inland?

  _____

3. What is Japan's chief crop? _____

4. Does Japan have more farm land or forest land? _____

5. Is the population density of Japan higher in the farming areas or the

  industrial areas? _____

6. What products are found near Sapporo? _____

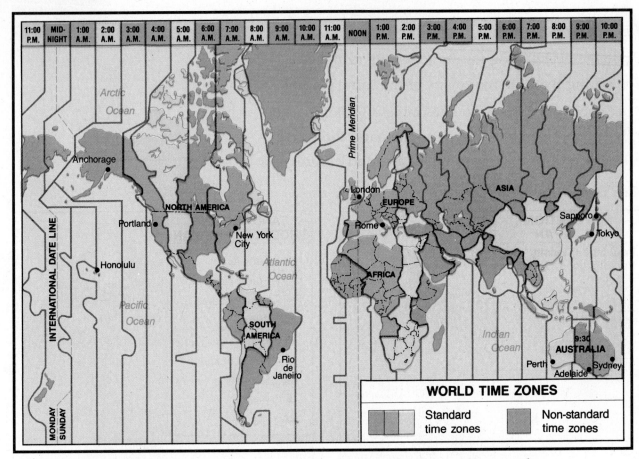

11:00 P.M.	MID-NIGHT	1:00 A.M.	2:00 A.M.	3:00 A.M.	4:00 A.M.	5:00 A.M.	6:00 A.M.	7:00 A.M.	8:00 A.M.	9:00 A.M.	10:00 A.M.	11:00 A.M.	NOON	1:00 P.M.	2:00 P.M.	3:00 P.M.	4:00 P.M.	5:00 P.M.	6:00 P.M.	7:00 P.M.	8:00 P.M.	9:00 P.M.	10:00 P.M.

WORLD TIME ZONES

Standard time zones

Non-standard time zones

Earth makes one complete turn, or rotation, every 24 hours. Since only half of Earth receives light from the sun at a time, it is not the same time everywhere on Earth. Earth is divided into 24 **standard time zones**, one time zone for each hour in the day.

Look at the time zone map above. The time in each zone is different by one hour from the zone next to it. Earth rotates toward the east. So as you travel west, the time is one hour earlier every time you cross into a new time zone. As you travel east, the time is one hour later.

Find London on the Prime Meridian (0 degrees). It is in the time zone labeled NOON. Now find Rome. It is one time zone east of London, so the time is one hour later. When it is 12:00 noon in London, it is 1:00 P.M. in Rome. Now find Rio de Janeiro. It is three time zones west of London, so the time is three hours earlier. When it is 12:00 noon in London, it is 9:00 A.M. in Rio de Janeiro.

Find New York City. How many time zones is it from London? Which direction is it from London? What time is it in New York City when it is 12:00 noon in London? It is 7 A.M. in New York City.

Notice that the time zones often follow political boundaries. This keeps places in one state, country, or area all in the same time zone. Some places around the world do not observe standard time zones and use different times. Find central Australia on the map. Notice that in Adelaide it is 9:30 when it is 8:00 in Perth.

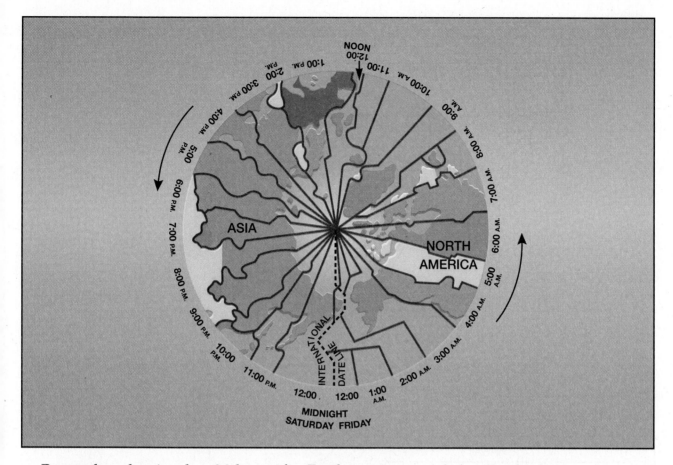

Remember that it takes 24 hours for Earth to rotate, and that Earth rotates toward the east. If you traveled west around Earth for 24 hours, you would set your watch back every time you entered a new time zone. When you arrived at home, your watch would show the same hour as when you left. But it would actually be 24 hours later—the next day.

Find the **International Date Line** on the drawing above. This imaginary line, at about 180° longitude, separates one day from the next. The time of day is the same on both sides of the line. But west of the line it is one day later than it is to the east. If it is midnight Sunday on the east side of the line, it is midnight Monday on the west side of the line.

Notice that the International Date Line does not follow the 180° line of longitude exactly. It goes around various countries to keep places in one political area in the same time zone and day.

Find Portland, Oregon, on the map on page 70. Suppose you start traveling west from Portland at 4:00 A.M. Friday morning. It is midnight at the Date Line. On the east side it is midnight Friday. But on the west side it is midnight Saturday. After you cross the Date Line, you enter late Saturday night. You actually miss one day, almost all of Friday. Farther west of the Date Line it is late evening on Saturday. In Sapporo it is 9:00 P.M. Saturday.

► Asia is west of the International Date Line. North America is east of the International Date Line. Look at the drawing above. If it is Monday in Asia, what day is it in North America?

► Look at the map on page 70. If it is 3:00 P.M. on Tuesday in Anchorage, Alaska, what is the day and time in Sydney, Australia?

Reading a Time Zone Map

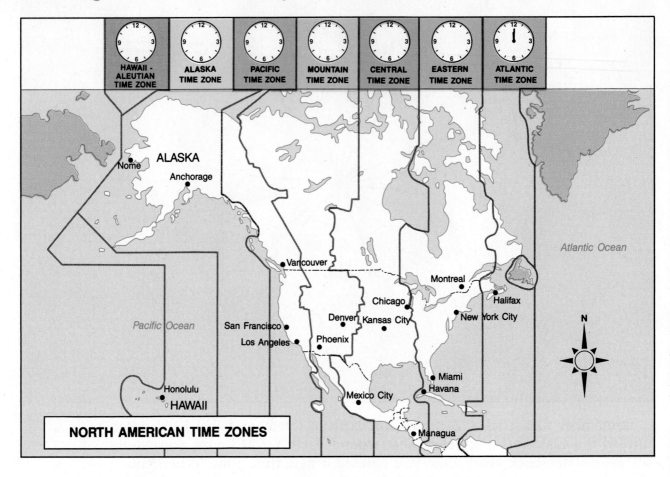

1. Lightly color the time zones. Match the colors at the top of the map. Follow the lines along state boundaries or physical features.

2. It is 12:00 noon in the Atlantic Time Zone. Write the correct times on the clocks for the other time zones. Remember, the time is one hour earlier as you travel west.

3. If it is 8:00 A.M. in Los Angeles, what time is it in each city listed below?

   a. Vancouver _____   e. Miami _____

   b. Kansas City _____   f. Denver _____

   c. Honolulu _____   g. New York City _____

   d. Anchorage _____   h. Halifax _____

4. The World Series is at 6:00 P.M. in New York City. What time is it in each city listed below?

   a. Montreal _____   d. Phoenix _____

   b. Mexico City _____   e. San Francisco _____

   c. Nome _____   f. Honolulu _____

Mastering World Time Zones

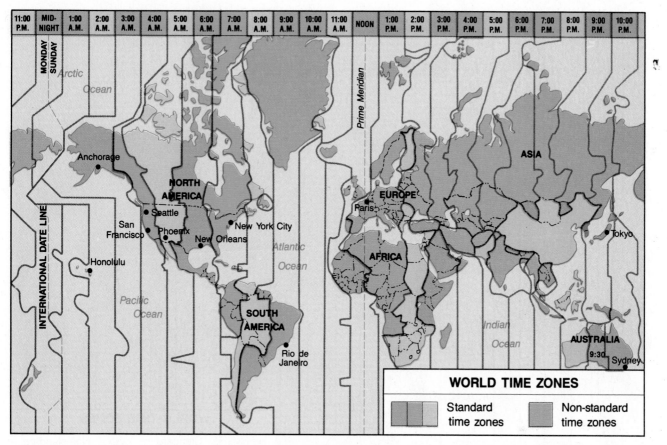

1. Which continents have a large area without standard time? Look at the colors in the map key.

   _____

2. How many time zones does each of these continents have?

   a. Africa _____   b. South America _____

3. If you go from Tokyo to Sydney, how many time zones do you cross?

   _____

4. If you go from Seattle to Rio de Janeiro, how many time zones do you cross? _____

5. If you go from Honolulu to New Orleans, how many time zones do you cross? _____

6. It is 7:00 A.M. in Phoenix. What time is it in Paris? _____

7. It is 3:00 P.M. in Rio de Janeiro. What time is it in San Francisco?

   _____

8. Suppose you fly from Anchorage to New York City. Do you move your watch ahead or back? _____ How many hours? _____

Mastering World Time Zones

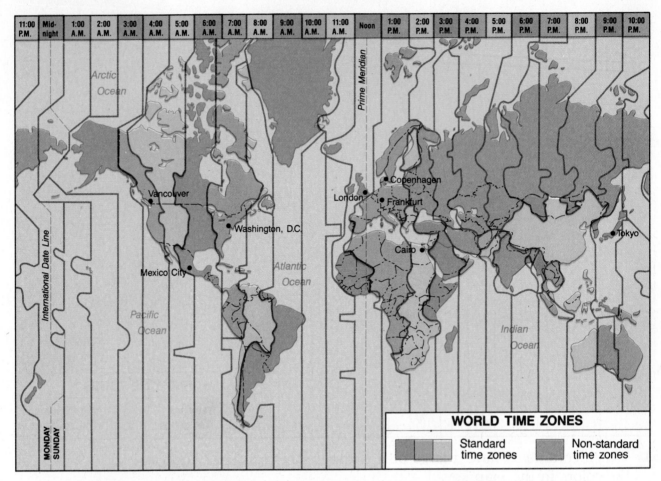

| 11:00 P.M. | Mid-night | 1:00 A.M. | 2:00 A.M. | 3:00 A.M. | 4:00 A.M. | 5:00 A.M. | 6:00 A.M. | 7:00 A.M. | 8:00 A.M. | 9:00 A.M. | 10:00 A.M. | 11:00 A.M. | Noon | 1:00 P.M. | 2:00 P.M. | 3:00 P.M. | 4:00 P.M. | 5:00 P.M. | 6:00 P.M. | 7:00 P.M. | 8:00 P.M. | 9:00 P.M. | 10:00 P.M. |

WORLD TIME ZONES

Standard time zones — Non-standard time zones

1. You are planning trips from London to various places around the world.
   Finish the chart below. Write the direction from London to each city.
   Then write whether you set your watch ahead (+) or back (−), and by
   how many hours. The first one is done for you.

From London to	Direction	Set Watch	How Many Hours
a. Frankfurt	east	+	1
b. Cairo	_____	___	_____
c. Tokyo	_____	___	_____
d. Mexico City	_____	___	_____
e. Washington, D.C.	_____	___	_____
f. Copenhagen	_____	___	_____
g. Vancouver	_____	___	_____

2. If it is 12:01 P.M. Tuesday in Frankfurt, what time and day is it

   halfway around the world? _____

Skill Check

Vocabulary Check   **standard time zones**   **International Date Line**

Write the words that best complete each sentence.

1. Earth has 24 _____.

2. When you go west across the _____
   it is suddenly tomorrow, and you lose a day.

Map Check

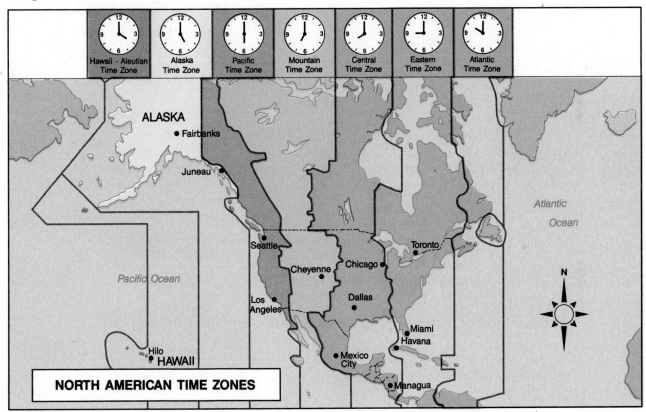

NORTH AMERICAN TIME ZONES

1. Dallas is in the _____ Time Zone.

2. Seattle is in the _____ Time Zone.

3. Toronto is in the _____ Time Zone.

4. Fairbanks is in the _____ Time Zone.

5. The President gave a speech at 9:00 P.M. Eastern Time. What time was it
   in these cities?

   a. Los Angeles _____   d. Havana _____

   b. Chicago _____   e. Cheyenne _____

   c. Hilo _____   f . Juneau _____

Geography Themes Up Close

Regions are places that are similar in one or more ways. Geographers categorize areas into regions based on one feature, such as the climate or type of government. They also recognize regions by a number of features, such as landforms, soil, language, history, and culture.

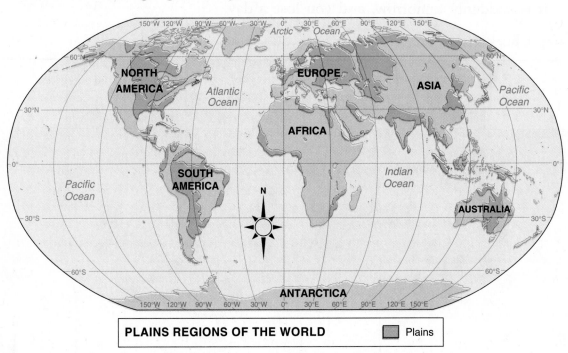

PLAINS REGIONS OF THE WORLD   ▢ Plains

1. What kind of feature—physical or human—describes this region?

_____

2. Which continent has no plains?

_____

3. In what part of South America are plains mostly located?

_____

4. In what two ways might plains regions differ from mountain regions of the world?

_____

_____

_____

_____

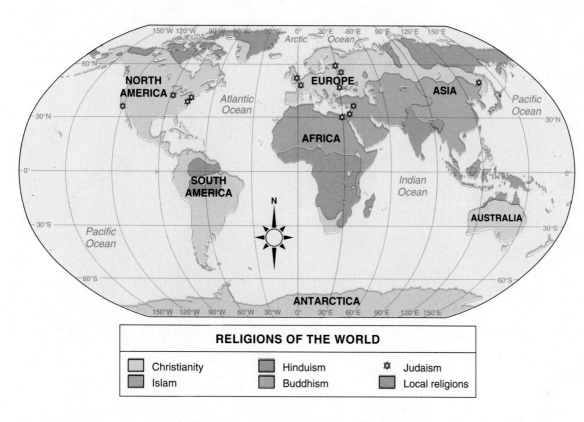

RELIGIONS OF THE WORLD

- Christianity
- Islam
- Hinduism
- Buddhism
- ✡ Judaism
- Local religions

5. What kind of feature—physical or human—describes the regions on this map?

_____

6. In what parts of the world is Islam a major religion?

_____

_____

7. What is the major religion of North America?

_____

8. In what parts of the world is Judaism practiced?

_____

9. Why might knowing the major religion of a region help you understand more about the region?

_____

_____

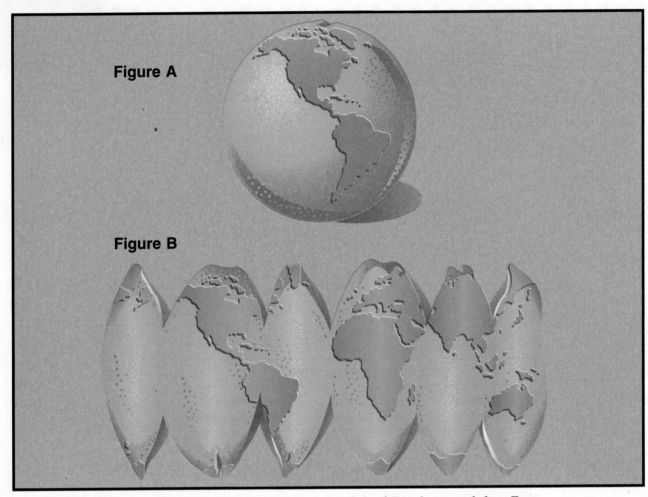

Figure A

Figure B

Since Earth is a sphere, the most accurate model of Earth is a globe. But often it is more useful to have a flat map of Earth. **Cartographers**—people who make maps—have made many flat maps of Earth.

Making a flat map of spherical Earth is not an easy task. To understand why, look at Figure A, which shows an orange made into a globe. Now imagine peeling the curved surface off the orange and making it lie flat. To do this, you need to stretch and tear the orange peel. Figure B shows the results. This action—taking a curved surface and forcing it to lie flat—is exactly what cartographers have to do when they make a flat map of the curved surface of Earth.

Look at the illustrations again. Notice how the shapes of the continents were changed when the curved peel was stretched flat. This change in a curved surface when it is flattened is called **distortion**. Every map of Earth has distortion. To draw a flat map of spherical Earth, parts of the sphere must be distorted, just as the orange peel must be distorted to make it lie flat.

Different maps distort Earth in different ways. Some maps distort the shape of continents. Other maps distort the size. The type of distortion a map has depends on its projection. A **projection** is the way in which a cartographer projects, or shows, the curved surface of Earth on a flat map. A cartographer chooses the type of projection to use based on the purpose of the map.

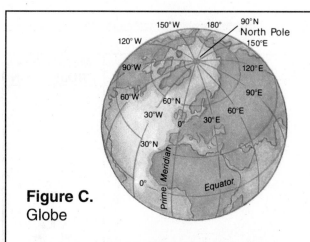

Figure C.
Globe

Figure E. Robinson Projection

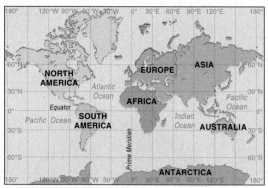

Figure D. Mercator Projection

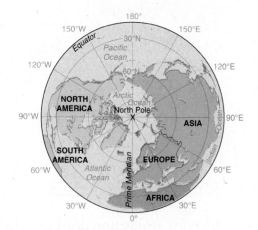

Figure F. North Polar Projection

There are many different kinds of map projections. A few of the most common ones are pictured here.

Look first at the drawing of the globe in Figure C. It shows the grid lines of latitude and longitude. As you look at each map projection, compare the grid on it with the grid on the drawing of the globe. This will help you see how each projection distorts the surface of Earth.

The map in Figure D is a **Mercator projection**. It is named after Gerhardus Mercator, a Flemish cartographer who lived in the 1500s. The Mercator projection is one of the most common map projections.

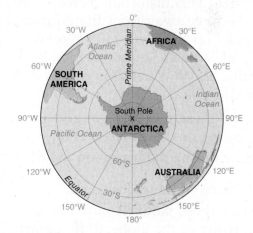

Figure G. South Polar Projection

The map in Figure E is a **Robinson projection**. It is named after the American cartographer Arthur Robinson. This projection is becoming more popular.

The maps in Figures F and G are **polar projections**. Why do you think these projections are called polar projections?

▶ Turn to the world map on page 74. What type of projection is it?

▶ Turn to the world map on page 60. What type of projection is it?

Reading a Mercator Projection

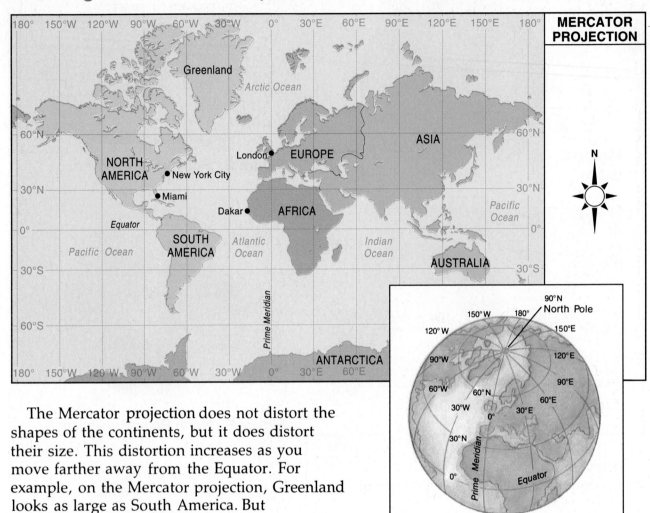

The Mercator projection does not distort the shapes of the continents, but it does distort their size. This distortion increases as you move farther away from the Equator. For example, on the Mercator projection, Greenland looks as large as South America. But actually, South America is much larger than Greenland.

1. Trace these meridians in green on both the Mercator projection and the drawing of the globe: 0° (Prime Meridian), 30°E, 30°W.
   How do the meridians on the Mercator projection differ from those on the

   drawing of the globe? _____

2. Trace these parallels in red on both the Mercator projection and the drawing of the globe: 0° (Equator), 30°N, 60°N.
   How do the parallels on the Mercator projection differ from those on the

   drawing of the globe? _____

3. An important advantage of the Mercator projection is that it does not distort directions. It is often used by sailors, who rely on accurate compass directions for navigation. Draw an arrow on the map from the first place to the second place. Write the direction of travel.

   a. London to Miami   _____

   b. New York City to Dakar   _____

Reading a Robinson Projection

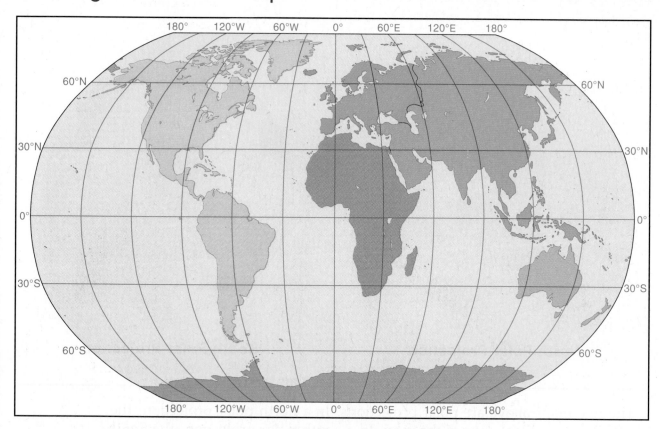

Every flat map of Earth has distortion. The Robinson projection is no different. It shows Antarctica as much larger than it actually is. Yet to many people, the Robinson projection looks more like a globe than most other projections. This is because the Robinson projection is a compromise of many map distortions. You can think of a Robinson projection as having many small distortions instead of a few large ones. The result is a map that looks very much like a globe.

1. Label the seven continents on the Robinson projection above: North America, South America, Europe, Africa, Asia, Australia, and Antarctica.

2. Label these four oceans on the map: Arctic Ocean, Pacific Ocean, Atlantic Ocean, and Indian Ocean. (Label both areas of the Pacific Ocean.)

3. a. Are the parallels on the Robinson projection curved or straight? _____
   b. How do these compare with the parallels on a Mercator projection?

   _____

4. a. Are the meridians on a Robinson projection curved or straight? _____
   b. How do these compare with the meridians on a Mercator projection?

   _____

5. Draw a conclusion. Why do you think the Robinson projection shows a small part of Asia on the left-hand side of the map, when most of Asia

   is shown on the right-hand side? _____

Reading Polar Projections

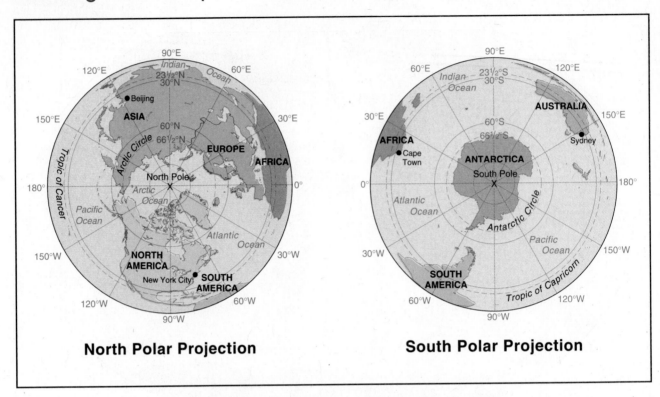

North Polar Projection

South Polar Projection

The two maps above are polar projections. In a north polar projection, the North Pole is at the center of the map. In a south polar projection, the South Pole is at the center. Polar projections usually show one hemisphere. Like all flat maps of Earth, polar projections have distortion. Polar projections are more distorted toward the edges.

1. a. Which hemisphere is shown on a north polar projection? _____

   b. Which hemisphere is shown on a south polar projection? _____

2. Label the Equator on each of the two maps above.

3. Usually, north is at the top of a map. In a north polar projection, however, this isn't the case. Remember, the direction north is the direction toward the North Pole. In a north polar projection, the North Pole is in the center of the map. If you go from any point on the map toward the center, you are going north. Imagine you are traveling from the first place to the second place. Which direction will you travel?

   a. New York City to the North Pole   _____

   b. the North Pole to Beijing   _____

4. The direction south is the direction toward the South Pole. Study the south polar projection above. Imagine you are traveling from the first place to the second place. Which direction will you travel?

   a. Cape Town to the South Pole   _____

   b. the South Pole to Sydney   _____

Skill Check

Vocabulary Check

Mercator projection   cartographers
Robinson projection   polar projection
distortion   projection

Write the term that best completes each sentence.

1. People who make maps are known as _____ .
2. Because all projections of Earth show a curved surface on a flat map, they

   have _____ .

3. The _____ was created for sailors in the 1500s.

Map Check

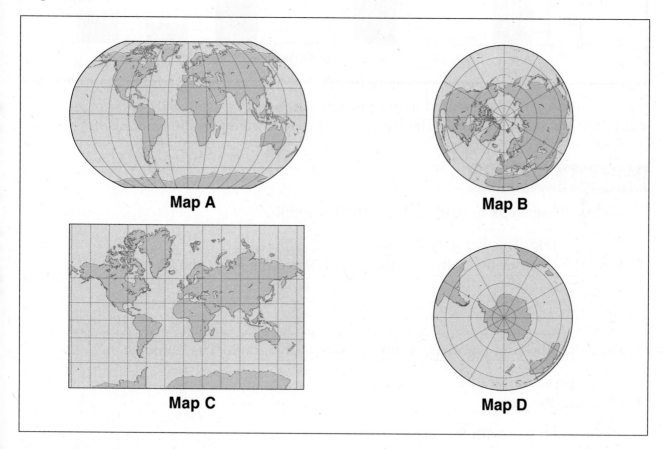

Map A

Map B

Map C

Map D

1. Identify each map projection.

   a. Map A is a _____ projection.

   b. Map B is a _____ projection.

   c. Map C is a _____ projection.

   d. Map D is a _____ projection.

2. Circle the projection that most closely resembles a globe.

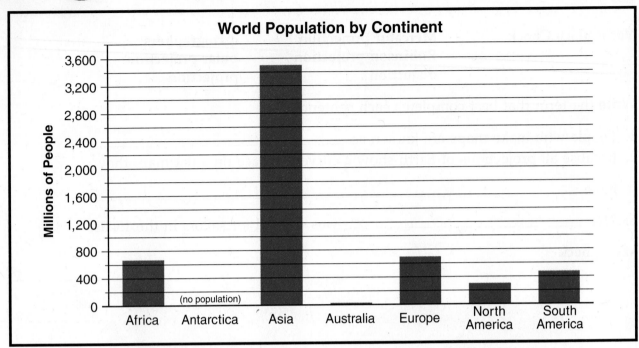

World Population by Continent

Information can be presented in graphs to make it easy to read. Bars on a **bar graph** stand for amounts. The bars make it easy to compare the amounts at a glance.

GRAPH ATTACK!

Follow these steps to read and use the bar graph.

1. Read the title. This bar graph shows _____.
2. <u>Read the labels at the bottom of the graph.</u> Name the areas shown on the

   graph. _____

   _____

3. <u>Read the label and numbers on the left side of the graph.</u> The numbers on

   the graph stand for _____.

4. <u>Compare the bars.</u>

   a. The continent with the largest population is _____.

   b. The continent with no population is _____.

   c. Estimate the population of North America. _____

   d. List the continents in order from greatest to least population. _____

   _____

5. <u>Draw a conclusion.</u> The population of Africa is slightly less than the

   population of which other continent? _____

Reading a Bar Graph

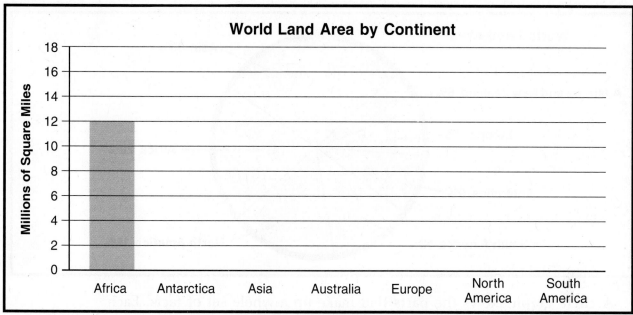

World Land Area by Continent

Millions of Square Miles

18
16
14
12
10
8
6
4
2
0

Africa   Antarctica   Asia   Australia   Europe   North America   South America

1. Read the title. This bar graph shows _____.
2. Read the labels at the bottom of the graph. Name the areas shown on the

   graph. _____

   _____

3. Read the label and numbers on the left side of the graph. The numbers on

   the graph stand for _____.
4. Finish the graph. Add bars to the graph to show the approximate area in
   square miles of the following continents:

Antarctica	5 million	Europe	4 million
Asia	17 million	North America	9 million
Australia	3 million	South America	7 million

5. Compare the bars.

   a. The largest continent is _____.

   b. The smallest continent is _____.

   c. Estimate the area of Africa. _____

6. Compare graphs and draw a conclusion.

   a. How do Africa and Europe compare in land area? _____

   b. Look back at the bar graph for population on page 84. How do Africa

      and Europe compare in population? _____

   c. Based on this information, do you think that Africa or Europe has more

      people per square mile? _____

Circle Graphs

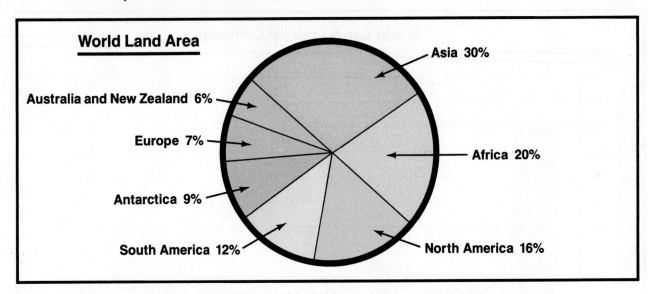

World Land Area

Asia 30%

Australia and New Zealand 6%

Europe 7%

Africa 20%

Antarctica 9%

South America 12%

North America 16%

A **circle graph** shows the parts that make up a whole set of facts. Each part of the graph is a percentage of the whole. All the parts together equal 100%. The circle graph on this page shows what percentage of all the land on Earth each continent includes.

GRAPH ATTACK!

Follow these steps to read the circle graph.

1. Read the title. The whole circle stands for _____.
2. Read each part of the circle.

   a. Which continents are shown in this graph? _____

   _____.

   b. What percentage of Earth does each continent cover?

   North America _____   Europe _____   Asia _____

   South America _____   Africa _____   Antarctica _____

   c. Which continent covers the largest area of Earth's surface? _____

   d. Which continent covers the smallest area? _____
3. Compare the parts. Write <u>larger</u> or <u>smaller</u>.

   a. Asia is _____ than Africa.

   b. Europe is _____ than Australia and New Zealand.

   c. Australia and New Zealand are _____ than North America.
4. Draw a conclusion. Europe and Antarctica together are the same size as

   what continent? _____

Comparing Graphs

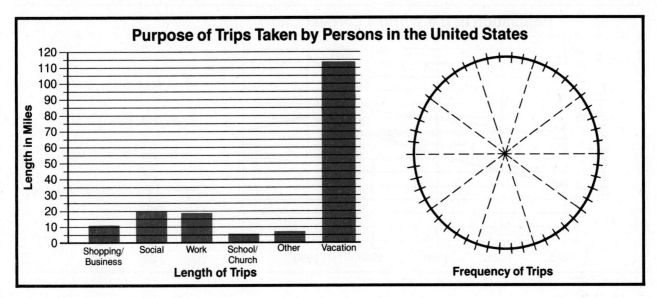

Purpose of Trips Taken by Persons in the United States

Length in Miles

120
110
100
90
80
70
60
50
40
30
20
10
0

Shopping/Business   Social   Work   School/Church   Other   Vacation

Length of Trips

Frequency of Trips

1. <u>Read the title.</u>

   a. The bars on the bar graph and the parts of the circle graph stand

   for _____.

   b. The bar graph shows _____.

   c. The circle graph will show _____.

2. <u>Finish the circle graph.</u> Each dotted section represents 10% of the circle.
   Use the information below to finish the graph. Color and label each part.

Shopping/Business 34%	Social 27%	Work 22%
School/Church 12%	Other 4%	Vacation 1%

3. <u>Read each graph.</u>

   a. The longest trip is for _____.

   b. The shortest trip is for _____.

   c. Most trips are for _____.

   d. The fewest number of trips are for _____.

4. <u>Compare the graphs.</u>

   a. Which trip is the longest and taken least often? _____

   b. What is the length of the trip which is most often taken? _____

   c. Not including vacation, what two trips are longest?

   _____

   d. Out of 100 trips taken, how many are long trips? _____

Line Graphs

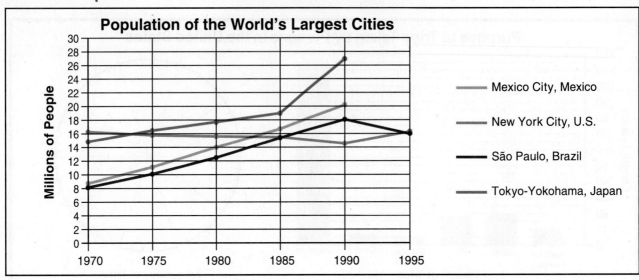

Population of the World's Largest Cities

— Mexico City, Mexico

— New York City, U.S.

— São Paulo, Brazil

— Tokyo-Yokohama, Japan

A **line graph** shows how amounts increase, decrease, or stay the same over periods of time. These general directions are called trends.

GRAPH ATTACK!

Follow these steps to read and use the line graph.

1. <u>Read the title.</u> This line graph shows _____.

2. <u>Read the numbers at the bottom of the graph.</u> What do these numbers

   indate? _____

3. <u>Read the label and numbers on the left side of the graph.</u> The numbers

   on the graph stand for _____.

4. <u>Read the graph key.</u> What does each line on the graph stand for?

   _____

5. <u>Finish the graph.</u> Use the information below to complete the graph.
   Population of Tokyo-Yokohama in 1995 = 28.3 million
   Population of Mexico City in 1995 = 23.5 million

6. <u>Compare the lines.</u>

   a. Which city had the largest population in 1970? _____

   b. Which city had the largest population in 1990? _____

   c. In what years did São Paulo and New York City have about the same

      population? _____

7. <u>Draw a conclusion.</u> The trend of the population of Mexico City is upwards. What is the trend of the population of New York City

   between 1970 and 1990? _____

Combining Line and Bar Graphs

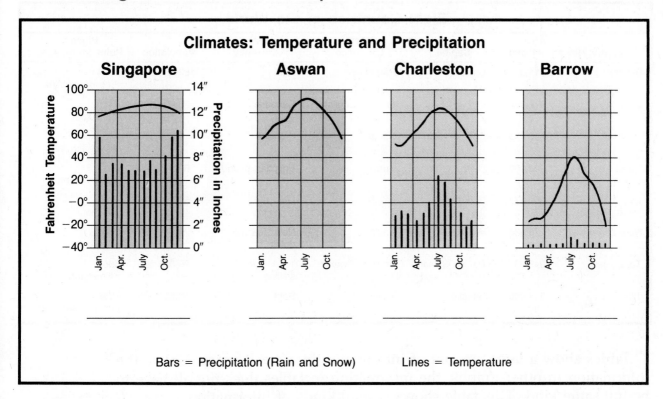

Climates: Temperature and Precipitation

Singapore   Aswan   Charleston   Barrow

Bars = Precipitation (Rain and Snow)   Lines = Temperature

1. Read the title. The graphs show _____.
2. Read the numbers along the sides of the graph. The numbers on the

   left sides indicate _____.

   The numbers on the right sides indicate _____.

3. Read the words along the bottom. The words indicate _____.
4. Compare the graphs.
   a. Which place has the greatest amount of precipitation?

   _____

   b. Which place has the lowest temperature? _____
   c. Which place has the least change in temperature over the year?

   _____

   d. Which place has the greatest change in precipitation over the year?

   _____

5. Draw a conclusion. Label each place with the climate zone that best
   fits it.

   Temperate = warm and rainy summer, mild and rainy winter
   Desert = hot and dry all year
   Tropical = hot and rainy all year
   Polar = cold and dry all year

Tables

Eight Countries of the World						
Country	Area (in sq. kilometers)	Capital	Official Language	Unit of Currency	Population	Highest Point (in meters)
Brazil	8,511,957	Brasília	Portuguese	Real	162,661,000	3014 Pico da Neblina
Canada	9,976,186	Ottawa	French; English	Canadian dollar	28,821,000	6050 Mt. Logan
Denmark	43,075	Copenhagen	Danish	Krone	5,250,000	173 Yding Skovhoj
Egypt	1,002,000	Cairo	Arabic	Egyptian pound	63,575,000	2637 Jabai Katrinah
Italy	301,278	Rome	Italian	Lira	57,460,000	4731 Mt. Blanc
New Zealand	270,534	Wallington	English	New Zealand dollar	3,548,000	3764 Mt. Cook
Tanzania	945,037	Dar es Salaam	English; Swahili	Tanzanian shilling	29,058,000	5865 Kilimanjaro
Thailand	514,000	Bangkok	Thai	Baht	58,851,000	2595 Inthanon Mountain

Tables show a large amount of information in a small space. Unlike the information in other graphs, the information in tables does not all have to be the same kind. This table shows several kinds of information.

TABLE ATTACK!

Follow these steps to read a table.

1. Read the title. This table shows _____.
2. Read the words along the top and the left side of the table.

   a. What countries are shown in this table? _____

   _____

   b. Name four pieces of information you can learn. _____

   _____

3. Read the table.

   a. What is the largest country in area? _____

   b. What is the least populated country listed? _____

   c. What and where is the highest point listed? _____
4. Draw a conclusion.

   a. Which are the two largest countries in area? _____ _____

   b. Which of those has the smaller population? _____

   c. Which has the greater population density? _____

Comparing a Table and a Map

Flights from Chicago				Time Zones in North America

Flights from Chicago

Departure Time	Arrival Time	Airline Flight #	Meal
To Acapulco			
8:55 AM	1:21 PM	AA 169	B
9:30 AM	3:15 PM	MX 803	LS
To Bermuda			
8:05 AM	3:40 PM	DL 88	BL
To Calgary			
10:00 AM	2:30 PM	UA 933	L
10:30 AM	3:00 PM	AC 833	L
To Mexico City			
1:50 AM	5:30 AM	MX 181	D
9:30 AM	1:10 PM	MX 803	L
3:45 PM	10:35 PM	MX 815	LS
9:50 PM	1:57 AM	AA 57	S
To Milwaukee			
7:00 AM	7:50 AM	AA 1241	
9:55 AM	10:31 AM	UA 559	
6:34 PM	7:16 PM	AA 205	
To Montreal			
7:10 AM	10:10 AM	AA 696	B
1:12 PM	4:12 PM	AA 286	S
5:40 PM	8:40 PM	AA 410	D

B - Breakfast   D - Dinner   DL - Delta Airlines
L - Lunch   AA - American Airlines   MX - Mexicana Airlines
S - Snack   AC - Air Canada   UA - United Airlines

1. Read the title.

   a. This table shows _____.

   b. The map shows _____.

2. Read the words along the top and the left side of the table.

   a. The flights from Chicago are to _____

   _____.

   b. What are two pieces of information you can learn about these

   flights? _____

3. Read the table key. What do the letters *AA* stand for? _____

   L? _____ *MX?* _____ *S?* _____

4. Compare the chart and the map.

   a. To which cities could you fly from Chicago without changing time

   zones?_____

   b. How many time zones do you cross to fly from Chicago to Calgary? __

   c. If you left Chicago at 10:00 AM, what time would you arrive in

   Calgary? _____

   d. When you arrive in Calgary, what time is it in Chicago? _____

   e. How long was your trip? _____

   f. How long is the trip from Chicago to Montreal? _____

THE WORLD

0   1000   2000 MI

0   1000   2000   3000 KM
(Equatorial Scale)

180° 160°W 140°W 120°W 100°W 80°W 60°W 40°W 20°W
80°N

GREENLAND
(Part of
Denmark)

A

U.S.
(Alaska)

60°N
Bering Sea

Hudson Bay

CANADA

Great Lakes

40°N

UNITED STATES

Mississippi River

BERMUDA

Atlantic Ocean

MORO

WESTERN
SAHARA

Tropic of Cancer

Gulf of Mexico

20°N

MEXICO

WEST INDIES

MAURITAN

CAPE
VERDE
ISLANDS

BELIZE

Caribbean Sea

SENEGAL

Pacific Ocean

U.S.
(Hawaii)

GUATEMALA
EL SALVADOR
HONDURAS
NICARAGUA
COSTA RICA
PANAMA

GAMBIA
GUINEA-BISSAU
GUINEA
SIERRA LEONE
LIBERIA
IVORY COAST

VENEZUELA

GUYANA
SURINAME
FRENCH
GUIANA

COLOMBIA

GHANA

KIRIBATI

Equator

0°

ECUADOR

Amazon River

WESTERN
SAMOA

AMERICAN
SAMOA

BRAZIL

PERU

TONGA

20°S

BOLIVIA

Tropic of Capricorn

PARAGUAY

URUGUAY

CHILE
ARGENTINA

40°S

180° 160°W 140°W 120°W 100°W 80°W 60°W
60°S

Antarctic Circle

80°S
60°S 40°W 20°W

80°W 60°W

WEST INDIES

Gulf of Mexico

Tropic of Cancer

BAHAMAS

0   300 MI

CUBA

Atlantic Ocean

0   300 KM

20°N

CAYMAN
ISLANDS

BRITISH
VIRGIN
ISLANDS

20°N

HAITI

**DOMINICAN
REPUBLIC**

PUERTO
RICO

JAMAICA

U.S. VIRGIN
ISLANDS

ANTIGUA AND BARBUDA

ST. KITTS AND NEVIS

HONDURAS

GUADELOUPE

DOMINICA

Caribbean Sea

MARTINIQUE

NICARAGUA

ST. LUCIA

ST. VINCENT AND
THE GRENADINES

ARUBA

NETHERLANDS
ANTILLES

GRENADA

BARBADOS

TRINIDAD AND
TOBAGO

COSTA
RICA

80°W

COLOMBIA

VENEZUELA

60°W

20°E 40°E 60°E 80°E 100°E 120°E 140°E 160°E 180° 80°N

Ocean

Arctic Circle

RUSSIA 60°N

Ob River

EUROPE

KAZAKHSTAN
Aral Sea
Black Sea
Caspian Sea
UZBEKISTAN KYRGYZSTAN
TURKMENISTAN
TAJIKISTAN

MONGOLIA

40°N

NORTH KOREA
SOUTH KOREA
JAPAN

AFGHANISTAN

CHINA

ISRAEL
IRAQ
JORDAN KUWAIT
BAHRAIN
QATAR
UNITED ARAB EMIRATES
SAUDI ARABIA
OMAN
YEMEN
DJIBOUTI
IRAN

PAKISTAN

NEPAL BHUTAN
BANGLADESH

Yangtze River

TAIWAN

HONG KONG

Pacific Ocean

LIBYA
EGYPT
Red Sea
Nile River

INDIA

MYANMAR
LAOS
THAILAND
VIETNAM
CAMBODIA

20°N

CHAD
SUDAN
ERITREA

ETHIOPIA

Arabian Sea

SRI LANKA

MALDIVES

PHILIPPINES

NORTHERN MARIANA ISLANDS

MARSHALL ISLANDS

GUAM

PALAU

FEDERATED STATES
OF MICRONESIA

CAMEROON
CENTRAL AFRICAN REPUBLIC

SOMALIA

BRUNEI
MALAYSIA

NAURU

CONGO
Congo River
UGANDA
RWANDA
BURUNDI
KENYA
TANZANIA

SEYCHELLES

SINGAPORE

I N D O N E S I A

PAPUA NEW GUINEA

SOLOMON ISLANDS

0°

TUVALU

ANGOLA
ZAMBIA
MALAWI
COMOROS

Indian Ocean

VANUATU

FIJI

NAMIBIA
ZIMBABWE
MOZAMBIQUE
BOTSWANA
MADAGASCAR
MAURITIUS

AUSTRALIA

NEW CALEDONIA

20°S

SOUTH AFRICA
SWAZILAND
LESOTHO

40°S

NEW ZEALAND

40°E 60°E 80°E 100°E 120°E 140°E 160°E 180°

60°S

ANTARCTICA

80°S

40°E

20°W 0° 20°E 40°E 60°E

60°N

EUROPE

Arctic Ocean

Arctic Circle

ICELAND 0 500 MI
0 500 KM

SWEDEN FINLAND

NORWAY

RUSSIA

60°N

ESTONIA
LATVIA
LITHUANIA
RUSSIA
DENMARK

Volga River

IRELAND
UNITED KINGDOM
NETHERLANDS
BELGIUM
GERMANY
POLAND
BELARUS

UKRAINE

KAZAKHSTAN

Atlantic Ocean

LUXEMBOURG
FRANCE
LIECHTENSTEIN
SWITZERLAND
CZECH REP.
SLOVAKIA
AUSTRIA HUNGARY
SLOVENIA
CROATIA
MOLDOVA
ROMANIA
Danube

MONACO
SAN MARINO
ITALY
ANDORRA
VATICAN CITY
BOSNIA AND HERCG.
YUGOSLAVIA
BULGARIA
MACEDONIA
ALBANIA

River
Black Sea

GEORGIA
AZERBAIJAN
ARMENIA

Caspian Sea

40°N

SPAIN
PORTUGAL

GREECE

TURKEY

20°W 0° ALGERIA TUNISIA MALTA 20°E
MOROCCO

CYPRUS
SYRIA
LEBANON
IRAQ
IRAN

Mediterranean Sea

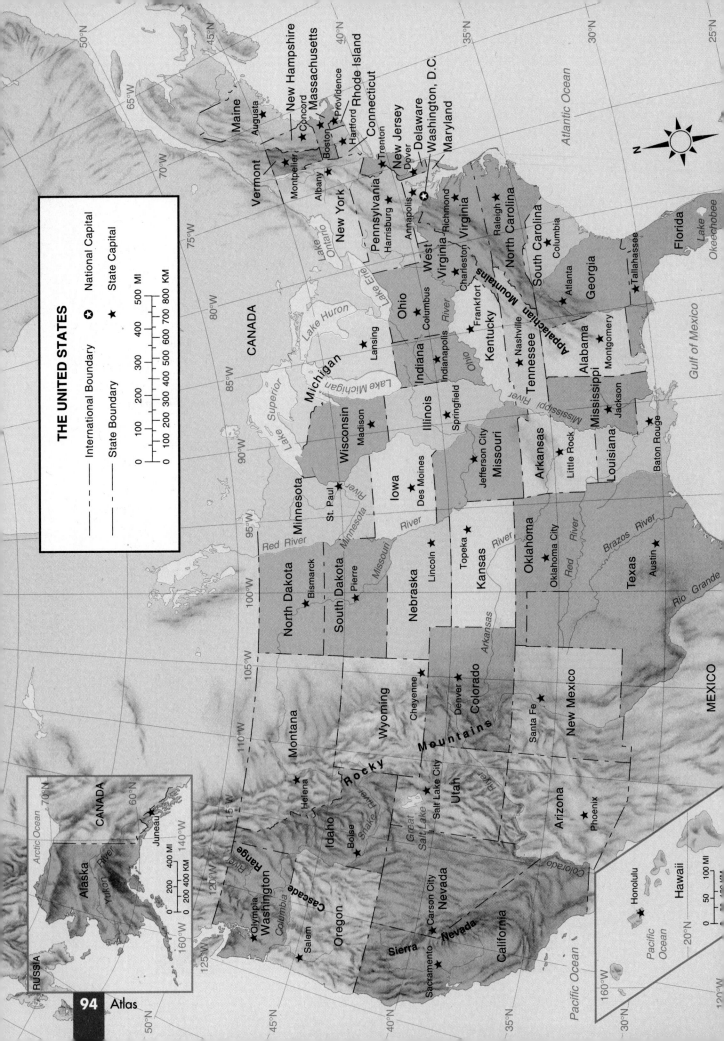

THE UNITED STATES

National Capital ✪
State Capital ★

International Boundary
State Boundary

0 100 200 300 400 500 MI
0 100 200 300 400 500 600 700 800 KM

CANADA

RUSSIA

CANADA

Alaska

Arctic Ocean

Yukon River

Juneau ★

0 200 400 MI
0 200 400 KM

Hawaii

Honolulu ★

Pacific Ocean

0 50 100 MI

Pacific Ocean

MEXICO

Gulf of Mexico

Atlantic Ocean

Maine
Augusta ★

New Hampshire
Concord ★

Vermont
Montpelier ★

Massachusetts
Boston ★

Rhode Island
Providence ★

Connecticut
Hartford ★

New York
Albany ★

New Jersey
Trenton ★

Delaware
Dover ★

Washington, D.C. ✪

Maryland
Annapolis ★

Pennsylvania
Harrisburg ★

West Virginia
Charleston ★

Virginia
Richmond ★

North Carolina
Raleigh ★

South Carolina
Columbia ★

Georgia
Atlanta ★

Florida
Tallahassee ★

Lake Okeechobee

Ohio
Columbus ★

Kentucky
Frankfort ★

Tennessee
Nashville ★

Alabama
Montgomery ★

Mississippi
Jackson ★

Appalachian Mountains

Michigan
Lansing ★

Indiana
Indianapolis ★

Illinois
Springfield ★

Wisconsin
Madison ★

Iowa
Des Moines ★

Missouri
Jefferson City ★

Arkansas
Little Rock ★

Louisiana
Baton Rouge ★

Lake Superior
Lake Michigan
Lake Huron
Lake Erie
Lake Ontario

Ohio River
Mississippi River

Minnesota
St. Paul ★

North Dakota
Bismarck ★

South Dakota
Pierre ★

Nebraska
Lincoln ★

Kansas
Topeka ★

Oklahoma
Oklahoma City ★

Texas
Austin ★

New Mexico
Santa Fe ★

Red River
Minnesota River
Missouri River
Arkansas River
Red River
Brazos River
Rio Grande

Montana
Helena ★

Wyoming
Cheyenne ★

Colorado
Denver ★

Rocky Mountains

Idaho
Boise ★

Utah
Salt Lake City ★

Arizona
Phoenix ★

Nevada
Carson City ★

California
Sacramento ★

Oregon
Salem ★

Washington
Olympia ★

Cascade Range

Sierra Nevada

Great Salt Lake

Columbia River
Snake River
Colorado River

Pacific Ocean

Glossary

absolute location (p. 4)   the specific address or latitude and longitude coordinates of a place

Antarctic Circle (p. 50)   The parallel of latitude 66 ½° south of the Equator

Arctic Circle (p. 50)   the parallel of latitude 66 ½° north of the Equator

bar graph (p. 84)   a graph that uses thick bars of different lengths to compare numbers or amounts

cardinal directions (p. 14)   north, south, east, and west

cartographer (p. 78)   a mapmaker

charts (p. 20)   facts shown in columns and rows

circle graph (p. 86)   a graph that shows how something whole is divided into parts

climate (p. 50)   the average weather of a place over a long period of time

climate zone (p. 50)   an area with a generally similar climate

compass rose (p. 14)   a symbol that shows directions on a map

coordinates (p. 29)   the letter and number that identify a grid square; the latitude and longitude of a place

degrees (p. 42)   the units of latitude and longitude lines

desertification (p. 62)   the spread of desert conditions to neighboring areas

distortion (p. 76)   the changes in a sphere that are shown on a flat surface, such as a map

elevation (p. 37)   the height of land above the level of the sea

Equator (p. 8)   the imaginary line around the middle of Earth that divides Earth into the Northern and Southern Hemispheres

Frigid Zones (p. 50)   the high latitudes that are cold all year

geography (p. 4)   the study of Earth and the ways people use Earth

globe (p. 8)   a model of Earth shaped like a sphere or ball

grid (p. 29)   a pattern of lines that cross each other to form squares

hemisphere (p. 8)   half of a sphere; half of Earth; the four hemispheres are Eastern, Western, Northern, and Southern

high latitudes (p. 50)   the Frigid Zones north of the Arctic Circle and south of the Antarctic Circle that are cold all year

human/environment interaction (pp. 5, 62)   the ways that the environment affects people and people affect the environment

human features (p. 4)   features of a place or region made by people, such as population, jobs, language, customs, religion, and government

inset map (p. 23)   a small map within a larger map

interchange (p. 28)   a junction on a major highway with special connecting ramps to allow vehicles to change roads without interrupting the flow of traffic

intermediate directions (p. 14)   northeast, southeast, southwest, northwest

International Date Line (p. 71)   an imaginary line at about 180° longitude where the day changes

junction (p. 28)   a place where two highways cross or meet

kilometers (p. 20)   a unit of length used in measuring distance in the metric system

latitude (p. 42)   the distance north or south of the Equator measured in degrees

legend (p. 14)   a map key, or list of symbols on a map, and what they stand for

line graph (p. 88)   graph that shows how something changes over time

location (pp. 4, 48)   the absolute and relative position of people and places on Earth

longitude (p. 42)   the distance east or west of the Prime Meridian measured in degrees

low latitudes (p. 50)   the tropics, or Torrid Zone, between the Tropic of Cancer and the Tropic of Capricorn that is warm all year

map index (p. 29)   the alphabetical list of places on a map with their grid coordinates

map scale (p. 20)   the guide that shows what distances on a map equal in the real world

Mercator projection (p. 79)   a projection that shows the compass directions between places accurately. Distance and size are distorted, especially near poles.

meridians (p. 42)   lines of longitude

middle latitudes (p. 50)   the Temperate Zones between the high latitudes and low latitudes where weather changes from season to season

mileage markers (p. 28)   small triangles and numbers on a map used to indicate distances along highways

miles (p. 20)   a unit of length used in measuring distance

mouth (p. 36)   the place where a river empties into a sea or ocean

movement (pp. 6, 20)   how and why people, goods, information, and ideas move from place to place

North Pole (p. 8)   the point farthest north on Earth

parallels (p. 42)   lines of latitude

physical features (p. 4)   natural features of a place or region, such as climate, landforms, soil, bodies of water, and plants and animals

place (pp. 4, 34)   physical and human features of a location that make it different from other locations

polar projection (p. 79)   a projection that is centered on one of the poles and shows the oceans and continents around the pole

population density (p. 57)   the number of people living in a certain area

Prime Meridian (p. 42)   the line of longitude from the North Pole to the South Pole and marked 0°

projection (p. 78)   a way of showing Earth's curved surface on a flat map

reclaim (p. 63)   to take back, such as land that has been flooded

regions (p. 76)   the basic unit of geography; areas that have one or more features in common

relative location (p. 48)   describing a location by what it is near or what is around it

relief map (p. 36)   a map that uses shading to show the elevation of land

Robinson projection (p. 79)   the flat projection that most closely resembles a globe. It shows less distortion than other projections do.

source (p. 36)   the place where a river begins

South Pole (p. 8)   the point farthest south on Earth

standard time zones (p. 70)   Earth is divided into 24 time zones. Each time zone has a clock time one hour earlier than the zone to its east.

Temperate Zones (p. 50)   the middle latitudes where the weather changes from season to season

Torrid Zone (p. 50)   the low latitudes, or tropics, that are warm all year round

tributaries (p. 36)   rivers that flow into larger rivers

Tropic of Cancer (p. 50)   the parallel of latitude 23½° north of the Equator

Tropic of Capricorn (p. 50)   the parallel of latitude 23½° south of the Equator

STANDARDIZED MIDTERM TEST

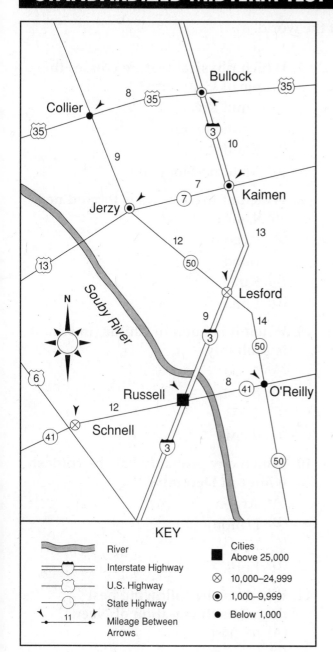

1. **Which highways do not cross the river?**
   - (A) 13 and 41
   - (B) 6 and 35
   - (C) 7 and 50
   - (D) 3 and 50

2. **What is the only interstate highway shown on the map?**
   - (A) 3
   - (B) 6
   - (C) 41
   - (D) 50

3. **In what general direction does State Highway 50 run?**
   - (A) North to south
   - (B) Northwest to east
   - (C) Northwest to southeast
   - (D) Southwest to northeast

4. **What is the shortest distance from Collier to Kaimen?**
   - (A) 9 miles
   - (B) 16 miles
   - (C) 18 miles
   - (D) 25 miles

5. **Which city is located 12 miles east and 9 miles northeast of Schnell?**
   - (A) Russell
   - (B) O'Reilly
   - (C) Lesford
   - (D) Kaimen

6. **What is the population of Jerzy?**
   - (A) Below 1,000
   - (B) 1,000–9,999
   - (C) 10,000–24,999
   - (D) Above 25,000

The map below shows an imaginary portion of the world.

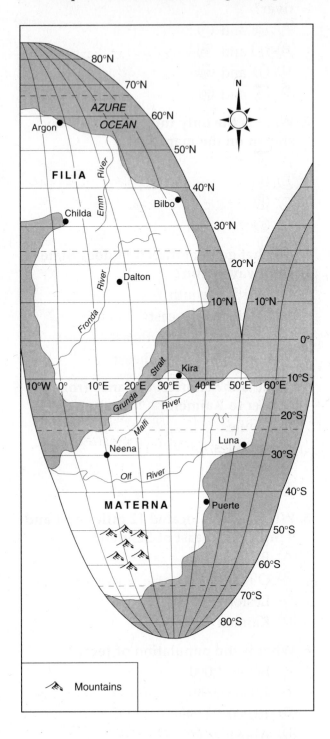

7. **Which physical feature crosses the Tropic of Capricorn?**
   - (A) Emm River
   - (B) Grunda Strait
   - (C) Malfi River
   - (D) Materna Mountains

8. **Which of these cities is located near 40°N, 40°E?**
   - (A) Argon
   - (B) Bilbo
   - (C) Kira
   - (D) Luna

9. **When it is noon in Childa, in Kira it is probably**
   - (A) 6 A.M.
   - (B) 8 A.M.
   - (C) 2 P.M.
   - (D) 6 P.M.

10. **Which city probably has the coldest winter in December?**
    - (A) Argon
    - (B) Dalton
    - (C) Kira
    - (D) Luna

11. **Which of the following best describes the location of Neena?**
    - (A) 0°, 30°E
    - (B) 30°S, 50°E
    - (C) 30°N, 0°
    - (D) 30°S, 10°E

12. **In which city does the sun set first?**
    - (A) Bilbo
    - (B) Luna
    - (C) Neena
    - (D) Puerte

Name _____

STANDARDIZED FINAL TEST

The three maps on this page show an imaginary country that has four states. Study the maps and answer questions 1–6.

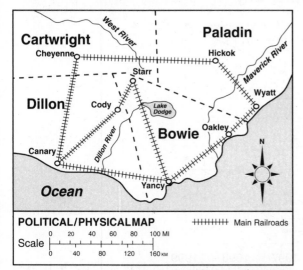

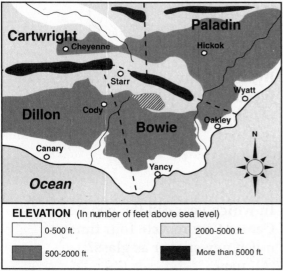

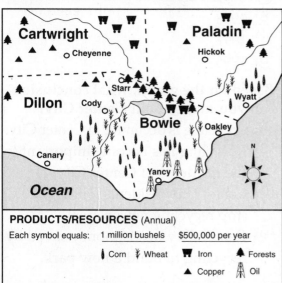

1. **What is the shortest distance by railroad from Cody to Yancy?**
   - (A) 75 mi; 100 km
   - (B) 130 mi; 210 km
   - (C) 220 mi; 355 km
   - (D) 380 mi; 315 km

2. **What product is most likely shipped out of Starr by railroad?**
   - (A) Iron
   - (B) Corn
   - (C) Wheat
   - (D) Lumber

3. **What might explain the lack of railroad service along the northern border of Bowie?**
   - (A) The area is very mountainous.
   - (B) The area has no mineral resources.
   - (C) The land is used to raise crops.
   - (D) The area is heavily populated.

4. **What is the elevation of Hickok?**
   - (A) 0–500 feet
   - (B) 500–2,000 feet
   - (C) 2,000–5,000 feet
   - (D) More than 5,000 feet

5. **What state is the largest wheat producer?**
   - (A) Bowie
   - (B) Cartwight
   - (C) Dillon
   - (D) Paladin

6. **Which statement accurately describes the land elevation along the railroad line from Cheyenne to Canary?**
   - (A) The elevation remains about the same.
   - (B) The elevation slightly increases.
   - (C) The elevation sharply increases and then decreases gradually.
   - (D) The elevation slightly decreases.

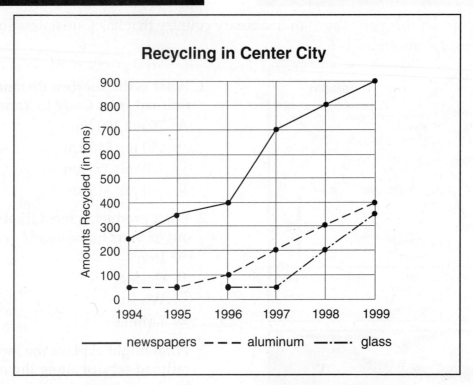

Recycling in Center City

7. In what year did the people of Center City begin to recycle glass?
   Ⓐ 1993
   Ⓑ 1994
   Ⓒ 1995
   Ⓓ 1996

8. Which of the following represents the largest increase in the number of tons of newspaper recycled in a one-year period?
   Ⓐ 50
   Ⓑ 100
   Ⓒ 200
   Ⓓ 300

9. Which of the following statements accurately describes recycling in Center City between 1996 and 1998?
   Ⓐ Total amounts increased substantially.
   Ⓑ Total amounts decreased substantially.
   Ⓒ Total amounts decreased slightly.
   Ⓓ Total amounts remained about the same.

10. By how many tons did glass recycling increase from 1996 to 1999?
    Ⓐ 100
    Ⓑ 200
    Ⓒ 300
    Ⓓ 400

11. In which year did the people of Center City recycle four times as much newspaper as glass?
    Ⓐ 1999
    Ⓑ 1998
    Ⓒ 1997
    Ⓓ 1996

12. Based on the graph, what conclusion can you make about Center City?
    Ⓐ Recycling is declining in Center City.
    Ⓑ Recycling has become important to the residents of Center City.
    Ⓒ Center City residents will probably stop recycling newspapers.
    Ⓓ Center City needs money saved by recycling to build a new park.

Answer Key

Geography Introduction

Page 4 Location Jackson Middle School is on a street in an area near many trees and houses.

Page 5 Place Answers will vary, but students might say it is a large city, located on hills near water; it has varied architecture and many buildings.
Human/Environment Interaction Answers will vary, but students should observe that clothes that are light-colored and lightweight, as well as loose-fitting, help keep the wearer more cool and comfortable in hot, dry climates.

Page 6 Human/Environment Interaction Irrigation provides the water necessary to grow crops when there is little rain.

Page 7 Movement Answers will vary, but students should recognize that both the truck and the barge are moving goods.
Regions Answers will vary. Students might answer that the region is marked by physical features—steep canyons and rock formations.

1 • Globes

Page 8 Question 1. south; north; **Question 2.** North and South America, Antarctica, Europe, Africa, Asia, Australia; Atlantic, Pacific, Arctic, Indian Oceans; Europe, Asia, Africa, Australia, Antarctica; Atlantic, Pacific, Arctic, Indian Oceans; North America, South America, Antarctica; Atlantic, Pacific, Arctic Oceans

Page 9 Question 1. Antarctica; Africa, Australia, South America; **Question 2.** Southern: Atlantic, Pacific, Indian Oceans; Northern: Atlantic, Pacific, Arctic Oceans; Southern: Australia, Antarctica; Northern: Europe, Asia, North America; Both: Africa, South America; **Question 3.** Northern; Southern

Page 10 1.–3. Globes should be labeled to match directions. **4.** North America and South America **5.** Europe, Asia, Africa, and Australia **6.** Antarctica **7.** Indian Ocean

Page 11 1.–3. Globes should be labeled to match directions. **4.** north **5.** south **6.** Antarctica, Australia **7.** Europe, Asia, and North America **8.** Arrow should be drawn to match directions; east

Page 12 1.–2. Globes should be colored and labeled to match directions. **3.** North Pole **4.** South Pole **5. a.** Northern and Western Hemispheres **b.** Northern, Southern, Western, and Eastern Hemispheres **c.** Northern, Eastern, and Western Hemispheres **d.** Northern, Eastern, and Western Hemispheres **e.** Northern, Southern, Eastern, and Western Hemispheres **f.** Southern and Eastern Hemispheres **g.** Southern, Eastern, and Northern Hemispheres **h.** Southern, Northern, Eastern, and Western Hemispheres **i.** Northern, Eastern, and Western Hemispheres

Page 13 Vocabulary Check 1. North Pole **2.** hemispheres **3.** globe **4.** continents and oceans
Globe Check 1. Globes should be labeled to match directions. **2.** North America, Europe, and Asia **3.** South America, Africa, and Australia **4.** the South Pole

2 • Symbols and Directions

Page 14 Frankfort, Kentucky to: Indianapolis, Indiana–northeast; Columbus, South Carolina–southeast; Columbus, Ohio–northeast; Richmond, Virginia–east; Nashville, Tennessee–southwest; Tallahassee, Florida–southeast

Page 15 Question 1. El Salvador, Nicaragua, Costa Rica, Belize, Guatemala, Honduras, Panama **Question 2.** Mexico, Guatemala, El Salvador, Honduras, Nicaragua, Costa Rica, Panama, Colombia **Question 3.** Guatemala; 13,845 and 13,045 feet; the height of each mountain is labeled **Question 4.** Cerro Pirre

Page 16 1. Map should be labeled to match directions. **2.** Colombia **3.** Costa Rica **4.** three **5. a.** S **b.** NE **c.** SE **d.** SW **e.** NW **6.** S

Page 17 1.–4. Map should be colored and labeled to match directions. **5.** Washington

and British Columbia **6.** Lake Winnipeg
7. Minnesota, Wisconsin, Michigan, and Ontario **8.** Akimiski Island **9.** NE; W
10. Minnesota and North Dakota

Page 18 1. Map should be labeled to match directions. **2.** Any four are correct: Eureka, San Francisco, San Diego, Acapulco, Salina Cruz **3.** Caribbean Sea **4.** Any four are correct: Caracas, Paramaribo, Recife, Rio de Janeiro, Porto Alegre, Buenos Aires **5.** Route should be traced and cities should be circled to match directions.

Page 19 Vocabulary Check 1. map **2.** cardinal directions **3.** compass rose **4.** legend **5.** title
Map Check 1. Map should be colored to match directions. **2.** Nassau to Havana–SW; Bridgetown to St. Vincent–W; San Juan to Charlotte Amalie–E; Dominican Republic to Haiti–W; Jamaica to Antigua–E; Trinidad to Tobago–NE

Geography Feature: Movement

Page 20 1. Sea routes, railroads, Trans-Siberian Railroad, seaports, inland waterways
2. Sea routes or the Trans-Siberian Railroad and other railroads **3.** The Trans-Siberian Railroad

Page 21 4. The northeastern part of Russia has no railroads and only the Lena River that could be used for transportation. **5.** China and Libya
6. The information shows how many people in each country have access to communication. It is likely that the fewer people that have access to communication tools, the less the movement of ideas and information.

3 • Scale and Distance

NOTE: All distances are approximate. Answers may vary slightly.

Page 22 Question 1. About 600 MI; about 960 KM **Question 2.** About 4,500 MI; about 7,200 KM

Page 23 Question 1. about 100 miles
Question 2. About 100 miles **Question 3.** the inset map **Question 4.** No, both places are not

shown on a single map. **Question 5.** Use the inset map to measure the distance between Ismailia and Suez. Use the map of Egypt to measure the distance between Suez and Asyut.

Page 24 1. a. about 150 KM; about 70 MI
b. about 300 KM; about 190 MI **c.** about 300 KM; about 190 MI **d.** about 450 KM; about 280 MI **2. a.** Oil field #5 to Tobruk **b.** Hofra to As Sidr **3.** to the coast; Answers will vary but may include the following: Oil can be transported on tankers; Cities on the coast may have industries or refineries.

Page 25 1. a. about 1,300 KM; about 800 MI
b. about 2,000 KM; about 1,250 MI **c.** about 1,000 KM; about 650 MI **d.** about 1,600 KM; about 1,000 MI **e.** about 400 KM; about 300 MI **f.** about 2,800 KM; about 1,700 MI
g. about 1,600 KM; about 1,000 MI **2.** about 10,700 KM; about 6,700 MI **3.** about 1,700 KM; about 1,000 MI **4.** about 1,400 KM; about 900 MI **5.** The Congo River trip is longer.

Page 26 1. Egypt, Algeria, Tunisia, Libya, Morocco **2.** Capital cities should be labeled to match directions. **3. a.** south **b.** Agadem
c. about 2,200 KM or 1,350 MI **4. a.** about 300 KM; about 200 MI; SW or S **b.** about 3,700 KM; about 2,300 MI; NE **c.** about 5,900 KM; about 3,600 MI; NE **5.** about 400 KM; about 300 MI **6.** About 10 days

Page 27 Vocabulary Check 1. a map scale
2. miles (MI) **3.** kilometers (KM)
Map Check 1. about 760 KM; about 460 MI
2. a. about 440 KM; about 270 MI **b.** about 1,150 KM; about 710 MI **c.** about 540 KM; about 330 MI **d.** about 330 KM; about 200 MI

Page 28 Question 1. U.S. Highway 49
Question 2. 13 miles **Question 3.** Biloxi
Question 4. Lake Pontchartrain or Lake Maurepas **Question 5.** Franklinton
Question 6. State Hwy. 26 **Question 7.** Bogalusa

Page 29 Question 1. Theatre for the Performing Arts, Municipal Auditorium; N. Rampart Street **Question 2.** Lafitte's

Blacksmith Shop, Preservation Hall, Pharmacy Museum, International Trade Mart **Question 3.** D-7, D-6, F-2 **Question 4.** French Market, Café du Monde, Pharmacy Museum

4 • Route Maps

Page 30 1. Map should be marked to match directions. **2.** 18 **3.** Port Colborne **4. a.** 3 **b.** Port Colborne **5.** Ridgeway **6.** 63 and 104 **7.** in Lockport

Page 31 1. Map grid should be completed. **2. a.** E.T. Seton Park **b.** Taylor Creek Park **c.** Queen's Park **d.** Sir Winston Churchill Park **e.** Kew Gardens **3.** Centre Island Park and Toronto Islands Park **4.** Riverdale Park, Taylor Creek Park, Woodgreen Park, E.T. Seton Park **5.** Warden Avenue **6.** Answers will vary.

Page 32 1. 139 **2. a.** 50 **b.** about 45 **c.** The highway curves. **3. a.** about 55 kilometers **b.** 80 kilometers **4. a.** Black Lake **b.** 20 and 265 **5. a.** 132 **b.** Answers will vary.

Page 33 Vocabulary Check 1. junction **2.** interchange **3.** mileage marker **Map Check 1.** Map grid should be completed. **2. a.** Deer Lake **b.** Trepassey **c.** Lark Harbour **3.** at Clarenville **4.** 360, 1, 410

Geography Feature: Place

Page 34 1. Physical features: Kanda River, Sumida River, Port of Tokyo; Human features: parks, gardens, government buildings, shrines, stock exchange, temples, museums, banks, universities, roads and theaters **2.** Imperial Palace, National Diet Building, foreign embassies, national library **3.** Answers will vary, but should offer some features from the student's town or city.

Page 35 4. Any of the following: Seine River, Island of the City, or St. Louis Island, gardens, parks **5.** Any three human features, other than buildings, shown on the map **6.** Answers will vary, but should offer examples based on the two maps. **7.** Answers should include two of the following: Eiffel Tower, Cathedral of Notre Dame, The Louvre, Arch of Triumph, or other famous buildings.

5 • Relief and Elevation

Page 36 Question 1. Vilyuy River **Question 2.** Ob River, Yenisey River, Lena River **Question 3.** low lands **Question 4.** Ural Mountains **Question 5.** Caspian Sea **Question 6.** Ural Mountains **Question 7.** peninsulas, plains, islands, plateaus **Question 8.** gulfs, oceans, seas, lakes, straits **Question 9.** Mt. Pobeda

Page 37 Question 1. purple or dark blue **Question 2.** yellow **Question 3.** to visualize the way the land looks and to tell its elevation **Question 4.** Moscow: 0–200 meters; Lake Baykal: 1,000–2,000 meters; Yakutsk: 0–200 meters **Question 5.** 200–1,000 meters **Question 6.** near the Caspian Sea

Page 38 1. a. Rocky Mountains; Columbia, southwest, Pacific Ocean OR Mississippi, south, Gulf of Mexico **b.** Andes Mountains; Amazon, east, Atlantic Ocean **c.** Urals OR The Himalaya; Amur, east, Pacific Ocean OR Indus, northwest, then southwest, Indian Ocean **d.** Alps, Urals, Carpathians, OR Pyrenees; Danube, east, Black Sea OR Volga, south, Caspian Sea **e.** Great Dividing Range, Murray, southwest, Indian Ocean **2.** the elevation

Page 39 1. These places should be circled: New Orleans, Cairo, Cape Town, Karachi, Stockholm, Buenos Aires, Melbourne **2. a.** 22,834 ft.; South America **b.** 15,771 ft.; Europe **c.** 29,028 ft.; Asia **d.** 20,320 ft.; North America **e.** 19,340 ft.; Africa **3.** Asia

Page 40 1. Mt. Ararat; 17,011 feet **2. a.** Pontic Mountains, northeast; **b.** Taurus Mountains, south **3.** eastern **4.** It decreases. **5.** about 800 miles **6.** about 350 miles **7.** Gulf of Antalya, Mediterranean Sea, Aegean Sea, Dardanelles, Sea of Marmara, Bosporus, Black Sea.

Page 41 Vocabulary Check 1. relief **2.** elevation **3.** source, mouth **4.** tributaries **Map Check 1.** Arghandab River, Lurah River **2.** Hari River or Morghab River **3.** Helmand River, Arghandab River, Lurah River **4.** in the far north and the far southwest

6 • Latitude and Longitude

Page 42 Question 1. a. Quito, Bogotá, Accra, Mogadishu, Padang **b.** 30°N: New Orleans, Cairo, Baghdad; 15°S: Brasília, Mozambique **Question 2.** 0°: London, Accra; 45°E: Baghdad, Mogadishu; 75°W: Montreal, Bogotá, Quito

Page 43 Question 1. Munster 52°N, 8°E; Leipzig 51°N, 12°E; Stuttgart 49°N, 9°E

Page 44 1. Meridian should be traced to match directions. **a.** west **b.** the Western Hemisphere **2.** Map should be marked to match directions. **3. a.** Mitú **b.** 0° **4. a.** 90°W **b.** 20°S **c.** 40°N **d.** 85°W **e.** 10°S **f.** 55°W

Page 45 1. Map should be labeled to match directions. **2. a.** 60°N, 25°E **b.** 50°N, 0° **c.** 60°N, 30°E **d.** 5°S, 145°E **e.** 50°N, 20°E **f.** 15°N, 75°E

Page 46 1. Map should be marked to match directions. **2. a.** NW **b.** W **c.** NW **d.** NE **3.** Atlantic Ocean **4.** Gulf of Mexico **5.** Bahamas, Florida, and Louisiana

Page 47 Vocabulary Check 1. Prime Meridian **2.** parallels **3.** meridians **Map Check 1. a.** Springfield **b.** Philadelphia **c.** Boulder **d.** Memphis **2. a.** 30°N, 90°W **b.** 40°N, 80°W **c.** 40°N, 120°W **d.** 30°N, 95°W

Geography Feature: Location

Page 49 1. label Venezuela on map **2.** label Bolivia on map **3.** label **a.** Lima and **b.** Cayenne on map **4.** circle Mount Aconcagua on map **5. a.** Bogotá **b.** Sucre **c.** Asunción **d.** Paramaribo **6.** Answers will vary, but may include that the Amazon River is located in northern Brazil, from the Atlantic Ocean west to the Andes Mountains. **7.** 14°S, 56°W **8.** Uruguay **9.** 16°S, 48°W **10.** Answers will vary, but may include that Guyana is located in northern South America. It is north of Brazil, east of Venezuela, west of Suriname, and south of the Caribbean Sea.

7 • Climate Maps

Page 51 Question 1. because it is found near the poles **Question 2.** Answers will depend on the students' location.

Page 52 1.–2. Map should be labeled and colored to match directions. **3. a.** Frigid Zone; high **b.** Temperate Zone; middle **c.** Temperate Zone; middle **d.** Torrid Zone; low **e.** Temperate Zone; middle **f.** Torrid Zone; low **g.** Temperate Zone; middle **h.** Torrid Zone; low **i.** Torrid Zone; low

Page 53 1. Singapore, Panamá, Accra **2.** Las Vegas, Aswan, Alice Springs **3.** Any 3 are correct: Buenos Aires, Charleston, Athens, Shanghai **4.** Any 3 are correct: Anchorage, Stockholm, Moscow, Yakutsk **5.** Barrow, Eismitte, Murmansk **6.** Chengdu, La Paz, Banff **7.** Polar **8.** Torrid Zone **9.** The Northern Hemisphere

Page 54 1. the climate of Europe **2.** cold temperate **3. a.** Helsinki; cold temperate **b.** Volgograd; dry **c.** Bergen; mild temperate **d.** Belgrade; cold temperate **e.** Dublin; mild temperate **4. a.** 60°N, 30°E; cold temperate **b.** 50°N, 30°E; cold temperate **c.** 50°N, 0°; mild temperate **d.** 40°N, 50°E; dry **e.** 40°N, 5°W; mild temperate **5.** 60°N

Page 55 Vocabulary Check 1. middle latitudes **2.** low latitudes, or Torrid Zone **3.** Frigid Zone **4.** climate **Map Check 1. a.** Madras, Bangkok, Singapore **b.** Chimbai, Qitai, Balkhash **c.** Guangzhon, Taipei, Tokyo **d.** Omsk, Irkutsk, Seoul **e.** Dickson, Nordvik, Ambarchik **f.** Konduz, Gar, Lhasa

8 • Combining Maps

Page 56 Question 1. north: Timor Sea, Gulf of Carpentaria, Coral Sea; south: Indian Ocean, Great Australian Bight, Tasman Sea; east: Pacific Ocean; west: Indian Ocean **Question 2.** Great Dividing Range: east; Great Sandy Desert: northeast; Great Victoria Desert: south **Question 3.** Temperate: eastern and southeastern coast and Tasmania; tropical: northern and southern coasts; desert: central and northwestern and southern coasts **Question 4.** temperate **Question 5.** Great Dividing Range **Question 6.** in the desert **Question 7.** The climate is harsh.

Page 57 Question 1. Brisbane, Sydney, Melbourne, Adelaide, Perth **Question 2.** uninhibited or under 2 per square mile **Question 3.** from 2 to 125 per square mile **Question 4.** from under 2 to 125 per square mile **Question 5.** temperate

Page 58 1. relief and climate **2. a.–c.** Answers will vary. **3. a.–c.** Answers will vary. **4.** Vienna, Budapest, Belgrade, Bucharest

Page 59 1. Moscow, London, Paris, and Istanbul **2.** St. Petersburg, Madrid, Berlin, Rome, Manchester, and Bucharest **3.** Stockholm, Helsinki, Marseille, Baku, Brussels, and Prague **4.** higher; Answers will vary but could include that people tend to live close to the cities. **5.** 25–125 persons per square mile **6.** cool summer, cold winter; Answers will vary but could include that it is harder for people to live where it is very cold.

Page 60 1. Africa and Asia **2.** Antarctica **3.** Antarctica **4.** Asia **5.** Map should be labeled to match directions. **6.** Conditions: too dry, too cold, too rough. Places: Answers will vary.

Page 61 Vocabulary Check 1. population density **2.** relationships
Map Check 1. a. Warm summer, mild winter **b.** Hot and rainy summer, hot dry winter **c.** Hot and dry all year **d.** Hot dry summer, mild winter **2.** Warm summer, cool winter **3.** It is wetter and cooler to the east. **4.** Tasmania

Geography Feature: Human/Environment Interaction

Page 62 1. severe desertification **2.** It is mostly severe desertification with moderate and slight desertification in some areas. **3.** Answers will vary, but students might state that it would be helpful to know which areas needed help, which areas should be helped first, and how to stop the desertification.

Page 63 4. 1900 to present **5.** the North Sea and some rivers **6.** northeast of Amsterdam at

IJsselmeer **7.** They have built canals. **8.** Answers will vary. Students might suggest that because the Dutch were draining water, there were probably some harmful effects on plants and wildlife that depended on that water, but overall, the interaction was beneficial to the people.

9 • Comparing Maps

Page 64 Question 1. north and northwest **Question 2.** farming and forest **Question 3.** farming

Page 65 Question 1. forest **Question 2.** forest **Question 3.** grazing land **Question 4.** grazing land **Question 5.** Calcutta–farming; Bombay – farming; Madras – farming; New Delhi – farming **Question 6.** Calcutta: copper; Bombay: no resources; Madras: no resources; New Delhi : sugar, copper

Page 66 1. olives, grapes, corn **2.** sugar beets, wheat, corn, rye **3.** It is forest. **4.** in the north **5.** It is farm land. **6.** olives, citrus fruits, wheat **7.** sugar beets, rye, oats, potatoes, grapes

Page 67 1. Any five are correct: Barcelona, Marseille, Lyon, Milan, Naples, Bucharest **2.** Any five are correct: Glasgow, London, Paris, Hamburg, Oslo, Stockholm, or St. Petersburg **3. a.** bauxite, grapes, wheat, iron **b.** olives, mercury **c.** mercury **4. a.** cotton, rice, citrus fruits, grapes, olives, bauxite **b.** corn, rice, wheat, grapes, citrus fruits, olives, gas, copper, mercury **c.** corn, wheat, grapes, bauxite, iron

Page 68 1. a. olives, hogs, sheep **b.** sheep, grapes **c.** coal, grapes **2.** grapes, hogs, sulfur, coal **3.** sheep, sulfur, goats, coal, poultry **4.** grapes, sheep **5.** Any three are correct: lumber, goats, sheep, coal, poultry, hogs, sulfur

Page 69 Vocabulary Check Answer b should be circled.
Map Check 1. a. the population of Japan **b.** land use and products in Japan **2.** along the coasts **3.** rice **4.** forest land **5.** in the industrial areas **6.** minerals, rice

10 • Time Zones

Page 71 Question 1. Sunday **Question 2.** 10:00 A.M. Wednesday

Page 72 1.–2. Map should be marked to match directions. **1. a.** 8:00 A.M. **b.** 10:00 A.M. **c.** 6:00 A.M. **d.** 7:00 A.M. **e.** 11:00 A.M. **f.** 9:00 A.M. **g.** 11:00 A.M. **h.** 12:00 noon **4. a.** 6:00 P.M. **b.** 5:00 P.M. **c.** 2:00 P.M. **d.** 4:00 P.M. **e.** 3:00 P.M. **5.** 1:00 P.M.

Page 73 1. Asia, Australia, and Europe **2. a.** four **b.** three **3.** one **4.** four or five, depending on the route taken **5.** four **6.** 3:00 P.M. **7.** 10:00 A.M. **8.** ahead; four

Page 74 1. b. southeast, +, 2 **c.** southeast, +, 9 **d.** southwest, –, 6 **e.** southwest, – , 5 **f.** northeast, +, 1 **g.** west, –, 8 **2.** 12:01 A.M. Tuesday

Page 75 Vocabulary Check 1. standard time zones **2.** International Date Line **Map Check 1.** Central **2.** Pacific **3.** Eastern **4.** Alaska **5. a.** 6:00 P.M. **b.** 8:00 P.M. **c.** 4:00 P.M. **d.** 9:00 P.M. **e.** 7:00 P.M. **f.** 5:00 P.M.

Geography Feature: Regions

Page 76 1. physical feature **2.** Antarctica **3.** in central South America **4.** Answers will vary, but students might suggest that since plains are flatter than mountains, they are more easily settled and farmed than are mountains, therefore having larger populations. There might also be differences in climate and temperature.

Page 77 5. human feature **6.** Middle East, North Africa, Bangladesh, Pakistan, central Asia, and Southeast Asia **7.** Christianity **8.** Europe, the Middle East, United States, and eastern Russia **9.** Answers will vary, but students might point out that ways of life in regions are influenced by the religion practiced there.

11 • Projections

Page 79 Question 1. They are centered on the poles. **Question 2.** Mercator **Question 3.** Robinson

Page 80 1.–3. Map should be marked to match directions. **1.** Mercator meridians are straight and do not meet. **2.** Mercator parallels are straight and do not curve. **3. a.** SW **b.** SE

Page 81 1.–2. Map should be labeled to match directions. **3. a.** straight **b.** They are the same. **4. a.** curved **b.** Mercator meridians are straight. **5.** to show that Earth is a sphere

Page 82 1. a. Northern **b.** Southern **2.** The Equator should be labeled on the maps. It is the outside line. **3. a.** north **b.** south **4. a.** south **b.** north

Page 83 Vocabulary Check 1. cartographers **2.** distortion **3.** Mercator projection **Map Check 1. a.** Robinson **b.** north polar **c.** Mercator **d.** south polar **2.** Map A, the Robinson projection, should be circled.

12 • Graphs

Page 84 1. world population by continent **2.** Africa, Antarctica, Asia, Australia, Europe, North America, and South America **3.** millions of people **4. a.** Asia **b.** Antarctica **c.** 300 million **d.** Asia, Europe, Africa, South America, North America, Australia, and Antarctica **5.** Europe

Page 85 1. world land area by continent **2.** Africa, Antarctica, Asia, Australia, Europe, North America, and South America **3.** millions of square miles **4.** Bars should be added to the graph to match directions. **5. a.** Asia **b.** Australia **c.** 12 million square miles **6. a.** Africa is much larger. **b.** Europe's population is slightly larger. **c.** Europe has more people per square mile.

Page 86 1. world land area **2. a.** Asia, Africa, North America, South America, Antarctica, Europe, Australia **b.** North America–16%; South America–12%; Europe–7%; Africa–20%; Asia–30%; Antarctica–9% **c.** Asia **d.** Australia **3. a.** larger **b.** larger **c.** smaller **4.** North America

Page 87 1. a. the purpose of trips taken by persons in the United States **b.** length of trips in miles **c.** frequency of trips **2.** The circle graph should be completed to match directions. **3. a.** vacation **b.** school/church **c.** shopping/business **d.** vacation **4. a.** vacation **b.** 11 to 12 miles **c.** social and work **d.** 49

Page 88 1. population of the world's largest cities **2.** years **3.** millions of people **4.** the population of a city **5.** Graph should be completed to match directions. **6. a.** New York City **b.** Tokyo-Yokohama **c.** 1985 and 1995 **7.** slightly downwards

Page 89 1. Climates: Temperature and Precipitation **a.** degrees of Fahrenheit temperature **b.** precipitation in inches **3.** bars and lines **4. a.** Singapore **b.** Barrow **c.** Singapore **d.** Charleston **5.** Singapore–Tropical; Aswan–Desert; Charleston–Temperate; Barrow–Polar

Page 90 1. eight countries of the world **2. a.** Brazil, Canada, Denmark, Egypt, Italy, New Zealand, Tanzania, Thailand **b.** Any four are correct: area, capital, official language, unit of currency, population, or highest point **3. a.** Canada **b.** New Zealand **c.** Mt. Logan, Canada **4. a.** Brazil; Canada **b.** Canada **c.** Brazil

Page 91 1. a. flights from Chicago **b.** time zones in North America **2. a.** Acapulco, Bermuda, Calgary, Mexico City, Milwaukee, Montreal **b.** Any two are correct: departure time, arrival time, airline flight number, meal **3.** AA-American Airlines; L-lunch; MX–Mexicana Airlines; S–snack **4. a.** Milwaukee, Acapulco, Mexico City **b.** 1 **c.** 2:30 P.M. **d.** 3:30 P.M. **e.** 5½ hours **f.** 2 hours

Sample Standardized Test • Book 3

Page 97 1. C 2. A 3. C 4. B 5. C 6. B

Page 98 7. C 8. B 9. C 10. A 11. D 12. B

Page 99 1. B 2. D 3. A 4. B 5. C 6. C

Page 100 7. D 8. D 9. A 10. C 11. B 12. B

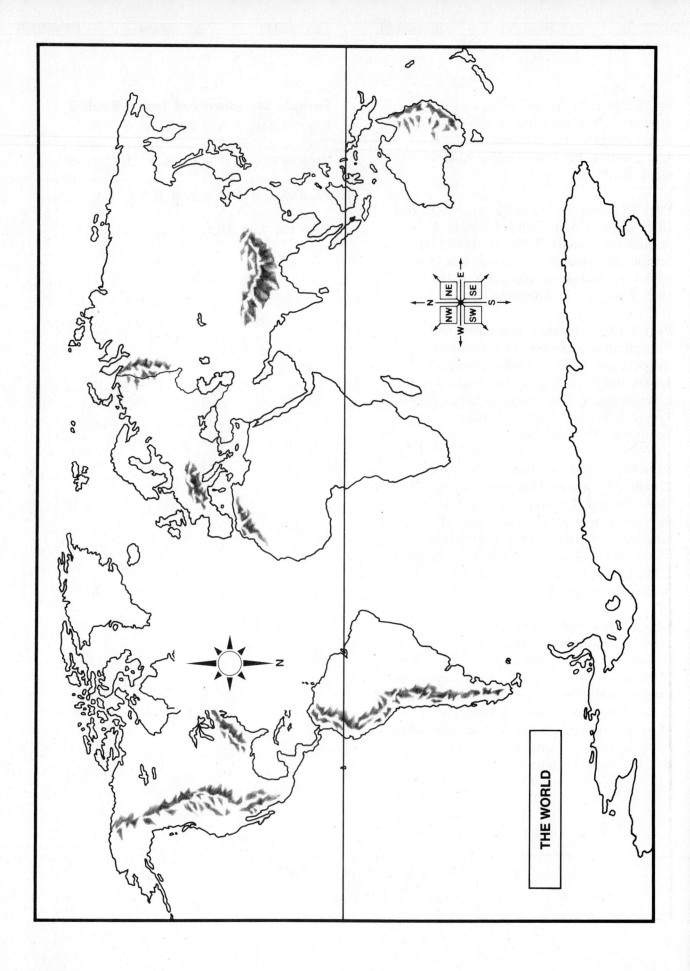

THE WORLD

Maps•Globes•Graphs   Book 3   © 2000 Steck-Vaughn Company

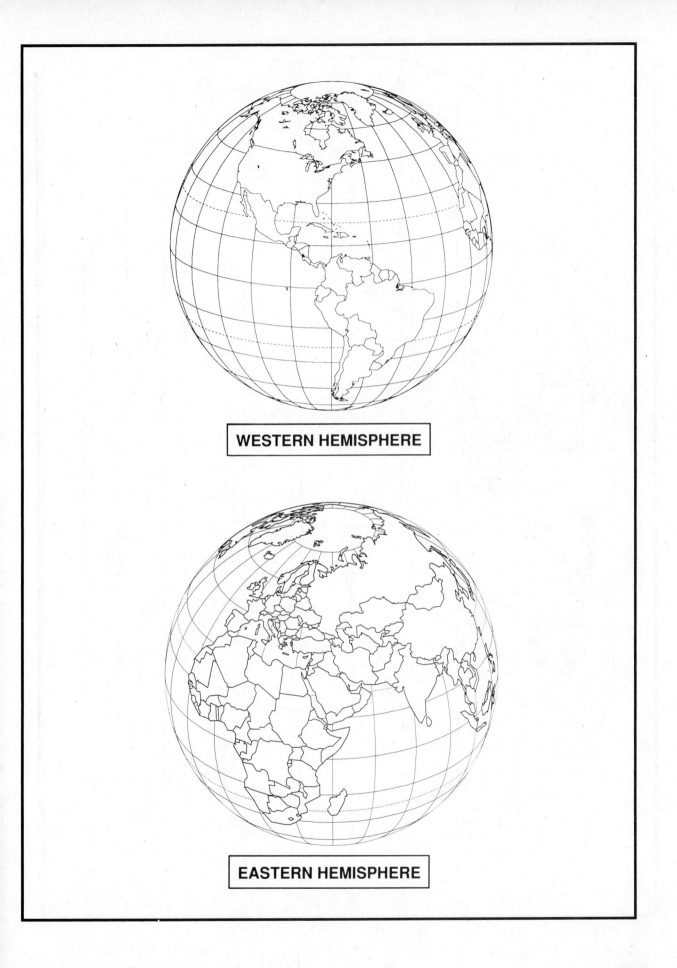

WESTERN HEMISPHERE

EASTERN HEMISPHERE

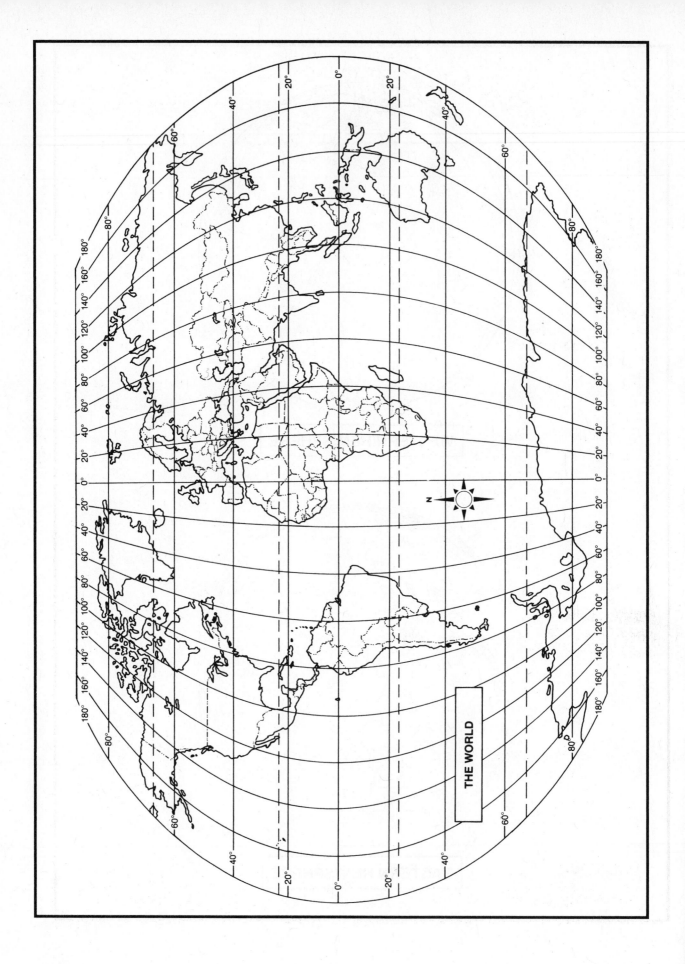

THE WORLD

Maps•Globes•Graphs Book 3 © 2000 Steck-Vaughn Company

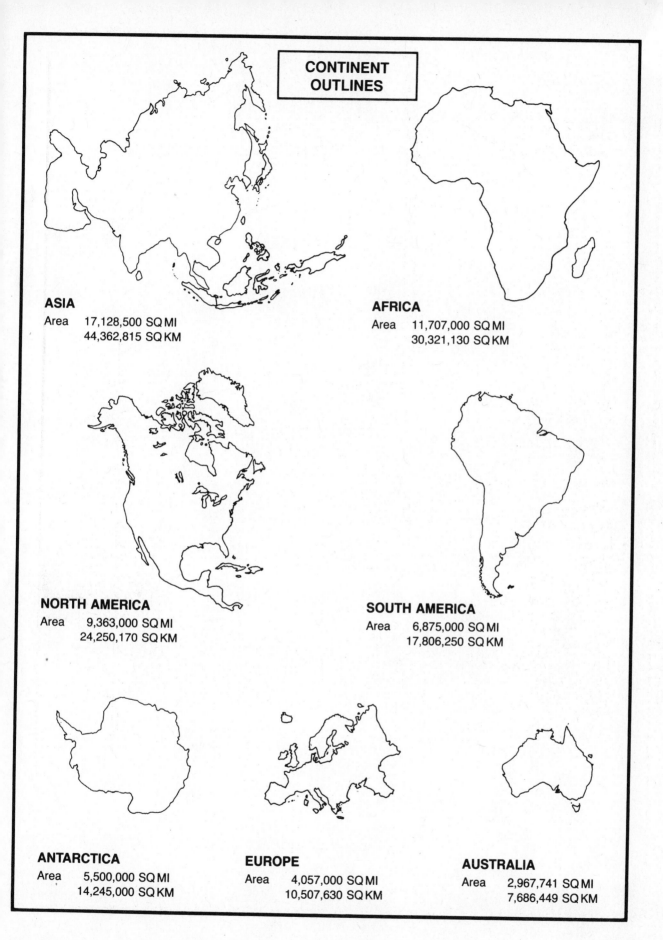

CONTINENT OUTLINES

ASIA

Area   17,128,500 SQ MI
        44,362,815 SQ KM

AFRICA

Area   11,707,000 SQ MI
        30,321,130 SQ KM

NORTH AMERICA

Area   9,363,000 SQ MI
        24,250,170 SQ KM

SOUTH AMERICA

Area   6,875,000 SQ MI
        17,806,250 SQ KM

ANTARCTICA

Area   5,500,000 SQ MI
        14,245,000 SQ KM

EUROPE

Area   4,057,000 SQ MI
        10,507,630 SQ KM

AUSTRALIA

Area   2,967,741 SQ MI
        7,686,449 SQ KM